DEBORAH RAE

A Holistic Sense of Home

A Quick Guide to Designing A Better Quality of Life

I welcome your comments, suggestions, photos, and success stories. For information about classes and other resources to design an enhanced quality of life with holistic interior design, please visit our website.

You can contact me at: www.Deborahe@InnergizedDesigns.com.

Disclaimer
(All That Legal Stuff)

Dedication

This book is dedicated to those who are on this amazing journey of discovery with me.
...May every day be filled with the joy of all the best in life.

Acknowledgments

This book would not have been possible without the knowledge and assistance of many people. I am deeply grateful to my friends and family for their patience, love, encouragement, and hours of review while this book was being written. Special recognition goes to my husband, Todd, for his computer support and photography. I also am indebted to my many teachers who have inspired me with their wisdom along the way. This includes my clients who have honored me by inviting me into their homes and lives and have taught me much within our time together.

Finally, I wish to express appreciation for the generosity of the talented designers and photographers who have allowed me to share their inspiring photographs included in this book. These include:

Brilliant Lighting, www.brilliant lighting.CO.UK

Juliette Byrne Limited, www.Juliettebyrne.com

Dowalt Custom Homes, www.DowaltCustomHomes.com

Kirtam Custom Curtains, www.Kirtamdesigns.com

Michael J. Lee, photographer, www.michaeljleephotography.com, and Janet Tosie Marena, designer, www.JTMInteriors.com

David Lauer, photographer, www.davidlauerphotograpjy.com, and Erin Iba, designer, www.ibadesignassociates.com

Lindsay Pennington, designer, www.LindsayPenningtoninc.com

Real Life Magazine, photographer, main architect: Nicholas Tye Architects, www.nicholastyearchitects.com, and local architects, John Doak Architects

Whit Richardson, photographer, www.WhitRichardsonPhotography.com

Contents

Section I

Background

1

Overview

New and improved design! Incredible return on investment (ROI)! Does windows! OK, reading this book will not clean your windows, but you will gain both practical tips on how to work with them and insight into why that makes a difference.

With the holistic design approach in this book, you can transform your daily experiences and more by tapping into what is already around you. If you feel you may be missing a piece - or peace - for the uplifting lifestyle and the quality of life you want and deserve, you may well find it at home.

Many of us who want and pursue optimal well-being, including the rejuvenating aspects of nature, overlook the pervasive impact of our homes. Home always has been a treasured concept across cultures and time, but now we live our lives inside our built spaces and in a high-tech, fast-paced world primarily disconnected from the natural world where we evolved. With our urbanized lifestyles, we average over 85 percent of our time indoors and about 67 percent in our homes according to the Environmental Protection Agency (EPA).[1] These lifestyle changes make the powerful influences of our homes more important to our well-being than ever before.

Increasingly over the past twenty years, many scientists, architects, and now designers have come to realize that there is a connection between some of our contemporary concerns and the sensory-impoverished uniformity, and related disconnect from nature so common in many of our man-made environments. Research links our physical and mental well-being to sensory interaction with nature and natural patterns. This effect has been proven to lower stress levels, increase productivity, enhance memory and creativity, speed healing, and even improve our relationships with others. If you cannot spend the time you would like outdoors, you can learn to bring more of nature and its rejuvenating power home.

This book was written to help you tap into the design triggers that big businesses, institutions, and specialty industries have effectively used for decades. These design triggers are also connected to the living healthier design trend, biophilia. With our daily environments, we set up behavioral patterns and internal responses that help or interfere with our well-being at every level. However, most of these interactions are largely outside our conscious awareness. Neuroscience indicates that's just how we are wired.

In the 1990s, a major illness kept me housebound. I was miserable. Desperate for ways to help me cope better, I studied the rapidly expanding research I was introduced to in graduate school: how our indoor spaces affect us. What I learned beautifully integrated with my former career and other love: educational psychology or facilitating learning and positive change including learning environments for student success. That was many years and many clients ago. Sharing what I have learned has been my passion ever since.

"Healthy home" has become a buzz phrase, similar to green and sustainable design a decade ago.[2] Healthy holistic interior design even sounds trendy, like a new design fad or maybe the latest rendition of the ancient art of feng shui. In my perspective, it is neither. My integrative holistic approach to healthier home interior design was born of personal need and developed over twenty years of study, research, and practical application. I am thrilled that the general concept is at last considered an emerging trend in interior design.[3] As often with an emerging field, there still is little comprehensive, practical framework available to guide us at home. After more than twenty years of research, training, and experience, this introductory book to holistic design is intended to give you that framework.

I love learning about the theory, the "why" behind something, but although steeped in research, this approach is also pragmatic. The holistic approach, tips, and techniques that I have found most effective over the past 20 years, I refer to as "innergized." Innergized reflects the constant interactions between our inner experiences (memories, emotions, goals, learning, sensory preferences, etc.) and our shared home, the physical world around us.

This book is divided into three sections: The first section is an overview of holistic interior design, including what it is and is not from an innergized perspective. Section two introduces you to some powerful tools in a holistic interior design toolbox plus some innergized tips on how to use them. Section three gives specific area-by-area examples of putting the holistic design principles and tips into place.

For those of you who want more of the specifics behind some of the research, check out the recommended reading and other resources found throughout this book. For those who are mostly interested in the nuts and bolts rather than the surrounding framework, you might skip directly to "innergized tips." Then go back to read about the why if you want more information to most effectively use the tips within your spaces or to add your own.

Some of what I will cover you may already know and already do. My purpose is to build upon what's already working for you and to help you minimize what is not working. I offer cost-effective practical tips and strategies from a wide perspective, then weave those together with the goal of leaving you eager to explore more on your own, feeling more alive and engaged in life, with a greater sense of well-being within and beyond your doors.

I believe holistic interior design is a joyful and empowering design approach for our homes and for our lives. By uplifting individuals - and individual families - with healthier, more productive experiences within our home spaces, the positive effects ripple out into our communities, uplifting us all. We are all part of a larger whole.

> "Home is more than a house. It is a sacred location, a place of aspiration and dreams, of learning and habit, of relationships and heart. Home is the geography of our souls."
>
> - Diana Butler Bass, *Grounded: Finding God in the World; A Spiritual Revolution*

The What and Why of Innergized Holistic Interior Design

Introduction

It is time for a new perspective. There are now countless interior design and decorating books and other resources offering various styles and design advice depending on the designer's perspective and aesthetics. This isn't another design style to improve the look of your interior. Creating healthier, life-supporting homes has been called a transformative interior design trend promoted by international companies, high-profile institutions such as the American Society of Interior Design (ASID), the Mayo Clinic, and holistic body-mind wellness guru Dr. Deepak Chopra.[3] My approach is a learnable life skill important for your happiness and well-being.

The field of interior design is just over one hundred years old and still evolving. The profession is a result of the industrial age. Interior design services emerged as the middle class in industrialized countries grew in size and status and wanted help selecting the domestic trappings of the wealthy to reflect their new prosperity. To fill the growing demand for upper-end home furnishings, and with the expanding ability to manufacture such products, large furniture firms branched into interior design, offering full house furnishings in many styles. This retail model flourished from the mid-1800s to 1914 when designers and decorators began establishing their profession.[4]

The shift to living in urban communities is also linked to the Industrial Age. Urban living, surrounded by an abundance of commercially available products and increasing isolation from the natural world, has gathered momentum ever since. Until that time, our lives and homes were closely integrated with our natural surroundings. For millennia our human development was shaped by our interactions with nature and the elements of our natural settings. These natural patterns have shaped who we are as a species and continue to influence us in multiple ways. Like nature itself, we humans appear to be a package deal, i.e., what affects us at one level ultimately affects us at all levels.

Our interior design choices may not make the difference between simply managing to get by and a good day or a good life, but do not underestimate the impact. Research and common sense indicate our environment can certainly tip the scales in one direction or the other! In fact, happiness and longevity researcher and bestselling author of the Blue Zone series, Dan Buettner, has said that environment is the single most important thing we can change to stack the deck in our favor for a long and happy life.

Too often, in our hectic twenty-first century lifestyle, instead of a healthy and uplifting place of belonging and rejuvenation, home is yet another source of daily stress, irritation, and unnecessary challenges. In fact, a 2014 Penn State study revealed that both men and women now experience more stress at home than at work![5]

"It is not the mountain that you must climb that wears you down. It's the pebble in your shoe."

- Muhammad Ali, professional boxer and social activist

Definitions

Here are some terms that you may have heard or read about but still may be unclear as to what they include or how they differ.

Holism is perhaps timeless in concept, but the term was coined by J.C. Smuts in his 1926 book *Holism and Evolution*.[6] Smuts emphasized the importance of dealing with wholes as integrated, interdependent systems rather than individual parts and asserted that a whole is greater than the sum of the individual parts. Radical in Western culture at that time, Smuts predicted that one day all science would accept this perspective. Holism began to be a more commonly accepted concept in the 1970s and is now accepted in many diverse fields such as medicine, ecology, and mechanical engineering. Holistic principles offer practical lifestyle options to meet our growing desire for enjoying a high level of vitality and well-being in rapidly changing contemporary life.

Holistic Interior Design focuses on the synergistic interactions of mind, body, spirit, and our interior spaces. The well-being of the occupants is, in turn, part of something larger still, including consideration for the physical environment and more. It is inclusive, with a focus upon what works for us in this life, so it cannot be separated from the world around us.

Core concepts and desired outcomes are similar to the holistic branches of other professional fields, but no standardization of the term or practice of holistic interior design exists. Many variations of approaches and training are found.

My short definition of holistic interior design is: an integrative person-centered approach to create home and work environments that nourish body, mind, heart, and soul while leaving the least negative impact on our communities and our shared home, Earth.

Biophilia recognizes a human need for ongoing connections with nature so strong that we cannot thrive as individuals or survive as a species without those connections. A growing body of research supports use of specific patterns such as natural lighting and healthy vegetation.

Biophilic Design is architecture and design that connects us to the natural world with the goal of contributing to an enhanced sense of well-being for the occupants of the space. Biophilic design also incorporates our individual cognitive, emotional and sensory preferences as important in creating an uplifting sense of place. Ultimately, biophilic design is more about restoring our connection to nature than specific techniques for designing indoor spaces.[7]

Geomancy is the study of earth energies and corresponds to a broad understanding of terrestrial influences upon life. Although the word is derived from ancient Greek, the practice of geomancy takes many forms and has been found in cultures around the world, sometimes dating back to prehistory.[8] Today, the three best known such culturally linked geomantic practices are probably feng shui from China, vastu shasta from India, wabi-sabi from Japan.

Ecosystem is "a community of living organisms in conjunction with the nonliving components of the environment, interacting as a system. Biotic (living) and abiotic (nonliving) components are interactive, linked through cycles and energy flows." Like all living things, human functioning depends on these supportive environmental connections.[9] I think of our individual home environments as personal ecosystems composed of interactive visible and invisible components including internal energy (such as sensory processing, emotions, and memories) and physical matter (such as furnishings and chemicals) linked together as one interactive unit. Healthy, uplifting homes include webs of mutually reinforcing and complementary relationships resulting in a whole system that's greater than the sum of the parts.

Your home ecosystem can fully support you and your loved ones or be an ongoing source of irritation and challenges, reducing your quality of life. The home as personal ecosystem concept acknowledges our biological roots as human beings and the influence of biophilic design which is credited as driving the current healthy home interior design trend.[3]

Green Design is the philosophy of designing physical objects according to the principles of social, economic, and ecological sustainability with the objective "to eliminate negative environmental impact … by utilizing natural resources that are biodegradable and reusable."[10] A "green" architect or designer attempts to safeguard air, water, and earth by choosing eco-friendly building materials and construction practices.

Sustainable Design also refers to the use of renewable resources for materials used in the spaces designed. The term sustainable design is sometimes used interchangeably with <u>eco-design</u>, <u>green design,</u> and <u>environmental design</u>. These areas of design all address the environmental impact of the built environment, but do little to consciously reconnect us to the natural world.[11]

Environmental Psychology is an interdisciplinary field of research-based study of the interplay between people and their surroundings and is sometimes referred to as research-based design. In diverse research over the past sixty years, primary focus has been on physical and mental health, social interactions, and productivity for people within man-made spaces.

What Innergized Holistic Design Is and What It Is Not

Innergized holistic interior design is "life beautiful" not simply "house beautiful." The focus is on you and how your spaces live, not on how they look. Aesthetics are still important, of course, but the litmus test is how well your spaces support the experiences and outcomes important to every aspect of your life.

For example, for some of us the minimalist trend is an antidote to sensory bombardment and a hectic pace of life, as represented in the photo below left. Others of us need more fullness in our spaces to be comfortable, as seen in this client's garage conversion, below right. Needing more living space, family heirlooms and mementos from travels now coexist happily with the family dog and energetic granddaughter in a room designed for comfort and active living. Neither is right nor wrong, except to the extent that it works for you at this point in life.

From an innergized perspective, holistic interior design

1. **Is NOT** about being "house proud" or attaching status to our belongings. The focus is on increasing awareness of how your daily experiences express and encourage (or discourage) what is important to you. It's about being more consciously alive in all ways in our physical world.

2. **Is NOT** a passing fad. Perhaps the most surprising thing about this trend is that it has taken us so long to consciously address the impact of our homes' influence upon quality of life.

3. **Is NOT** feng shui, nor any specific culturally linked system. Most indigenous cultures have a set of beliefs about how to best live in harmony within the natural world. Many such wisdoms are, at heart, common sense; others make sense within their particular culture and geographic area. Even feng shui, now the most recognized such system in our contemporary Western culture, varies in how to achieve that goal. Feng shui is complex with many schools and sometimes conflicting advice across those schools. To better understand the underlying principles,

I've studied many such systems and am certified in two feng shui schools. The approach in this book is all about you becoming more aware of how you affect your quality of life with design choices to support your own values, needs, and beliefs.

4. **Is NOT** dependent upon the good tastes, skills, or values of a select few, but is a life skill we can all (re)learn. It is spiritual in that your design choices consciously enhance more of the sacred in our everyday experiences. Your choices will reflect the beliefs that knit together your ideals, principles, and values that guide and motivate you.

5. **Is NOT** expensive construction, remodeling, or replacing furnishings that require a large amount of money, time, and energy. Even simple changes can make a big difference almost immediately. Positive change using holistic interior design can often be accomplished with simple, inexpensive strategies. Any changes you make are quality-of-life investments with great long and short term return on investment (ROI).

"Good health depends to a large extent on certain choices that we make that include... how we manage the environments in which we live and work."

- The New Wellness Encyclopedia

The Cost

Can you and your family afford NOT to have healthy, high-functioning holistic interior design choices for your home? Here are some ways that living without healthy, productive, uplifting home and work spaces can be costing you and your family.

Stress The Centers for Disease Control estimates that 80 percent of disease today is related to stress. Stress is linked to 75-90 percent of visits to physicians.[12,13] Lower stress at home, and you can lower stress levels beyond your doors, too. In one study, almost 90 percent of the women who made adjustments in the rooms where they spent the most time also reported reduced levels of life stress away from home. Recent Pennsylvania State University research revealed that both men and women feel more stress at home than at work.[5, 12]

One study revealed that the average American child reports levels of anxiety today higher than the average child under a psychiatrists' care in the 1950s. Educators have long known that environmental sensory over- or under -stimulation and other environmental "mismatches" are sources of lack of focus, learning disabilites, heightened stress, and behavioral problems in children.[14] Such reactions are not limited to the classroom or to our children!

Time and Energy Our lives are busier than ever with our jobs, school, and family life. Trying to focus on many activities, or even one thing for long periods of time, creates something called directed attention fatigue. Connecting with nature by looking at plants, water, birds, and other aspects of nature gives us the cognitive quick break that seems to renew our ability to be creative and focus effectively again, measurably lowering the number of errors and related frustration.[15] Some natural patterns, such as diffused and varied lighting, are linked to decreased stress, enhanced memory and creativity, higher test scores, and improved social interaction.

Money Clutter and disorganization crowd us out of our homes and garages and then we rent space to store items we no longer want in our homes. The U.S. Department of Energy reports that 25 percent of people with two car garages fill them with so much stuff that they can't park a car inside, and still nearly 10 percent of American households spend over $1,000 a year for storage space rental.[16] The average person on an average day spends thirty minutes to two hours looking for "stuff." And when we can't find what we need, we buy duplicate items, costing us even more time, energy, peace of mind, and money.[16, 17]

Clutter even has been linked with weight gain.[18] It is estimated that half of us diet at some point every year. While spending billions each year on diet and exercise books and programs, we keep gaining weight. And we keep the same lifestyles and the same daily routines at home.

What can you and your family gain with home and work spaces that support you?

- Time and energy for what you enjoy
- Peace of mind
- Better relationships
- Productivity, efficiency, creativity for enhanced bottom line
- More money for discretionary spending
- Fewer trips to the doctor and less spent on medication
- Physical, emotional, spiritual, financial well-being

All living things are dependent on their environments. We are not an exception. As a species, we now face unprecedented challenges to our health and the health of our shared home, Earth. Even low levels of pollution inside our homes are proven to contribute to epidemic rates of obesity, respiratory and other chronic and sometimes fatal diseases. Holistic design is a cost-effective investment in a healthy, uplifting quality of life. When your home is a healthy ecosystem well connected to the surrounding world, you can experience positive life results faster, with less effort and with less stress.

We can design a difference. For decades the research has been accumulating about how our homes and other indoor spaces influence our actions, interactions, habits, and health. The "what and how" has largely remained within lucrative business sectors such as health care, hospitality, retail, and government institutions, or remained within the halls of academia. But with the emerging buzz for designing healthier spaces,[2] a holistic approach to healthier interior design is finally coming home.

"This trend [designing indoor environments for positive mental and physical response] is the next big movement in human wellbeing." [19]

– Dr. Deepak Chopra

Section II
Tools

Design with Sensory Awareness

Sensory input can regulate our sleep-wake cycle, drive us toward healthy or unhealthy choices, affect our relationships, and impact our general well-being 24/7. The sights we see, the sounds we hear, and even how we move through our homes affect us. Everything. All the time. Even when we sleep, our subconscious is processing sensory information from the world around us. The physical world is literally absorbed and defined through our senses. Our daily experiences (physical, emotional, and mental) are shaped from our sensory interactions. And this sensory interaction begins before we are even born.

Human brains evolved to respond to stimuli from simultaneously received multiple sources. But research into how this works traditionally was considered one sense modality at a time. Today, multi-sensory perception has been widely studied in cognitive science and neuroscience.

Still, many questions remain about how we generate unified, coherent perceptions from the bombardment of electromagnetic waves, chemical interactions, and pressure fluctuations that form our impression of the physical world surrounding us. And, as incredible as they are, the standard list of five senses doesn't give our bodies credit for all the amazing things they do. Scientists indicate there are more than a dozen different ways we can sense the world around us.[20] In general, contrast and variety engage our senses and our attention. Varied sensory stimuli within our built spaces seems to be healthier for us than uniformity.[7, 21]

We now know that our emotions and our senses are tightly intertwined. Sensory cues emotionally connect us to specific places and people. Our emotional responses to sensory stimulus are fast, activated in less than a second, so are primarily too fast for conscious awareness. Our senses provide us with a rapid means to experience and interact with the world around us. That's the technical side of it. But science does not tell us how to apply these facts to our lives.

Awareness of sensory cues around us has been linked to an ability to derive pleasure in life as a whole. How many of us take simple physical pleasures for granted? Do you already fully notice the smells, textures, and sounds in and around your home? Sensuality is essentially how tuned in you are to your physical senses.

Designing with a holistic perspective is a sensory celebration. Let nature inspire you. What brings you comfort and pleasure in this world? When we pay attention in this way, we are more consciously alive, more awake, and more fully ourselves on every level.

Vision

While we are hardwired to seek sensory patterns in everything around us, much of traditional interior design has been focused on aesthetics, how a space *looks*. The following is a brief review of some visual patterns in interior design that you may know and already use in your decorating.

Visual Patterns in Traditional Interior Design

Balance is the arrangement of anything that creates a sense of visual equilibrium. Two basic types of visual balance are:

1. <u>Symmetric balance</u> includes a matched pair, two of the same thing. Symmetric balance is the easiest and most formal arrangement.
2. <u>Asymmetric balance</u> is more informal and dynamic and contains unmatched items. Asymmetric balance creates more visual interest and encourages activity more than relaxation.

<u>Visual weight</u> is what draws our eye and holds it longest. Many elements can make objects seem heavier or lighter than those around it. For example, dark/black objects seem heavier than clear or white objects.

<u>Focal Point</u> is where the eye naturally goes. The eye is drawn to color, light, movement, and visual weight. A large piece of furniture such as a bed, for example, can be the focal point in a room.

<u>Pattern</u> in design refers to the repetition of an element on a surface. Pattern adds interest in an otherwise boring area, but too much pattern can overwhelm a space. Pattern usually can be seen as individual elements, but if very small or seen from a distance, pattern can resemble texture.

<u>Texture</u> refers to how a surface feels or *appears* to feel. Texture affects the perceived size of a space. Shiny, reflective, polished surfaces, as in the shiny kitchen finishes on the far right, tend to make a room seem more open, spacious, and cooler. The matte textures in the left photo seem more natural, warmer, cozy, and touchable.

<u>Proportion</u> is how parts relate to the whole or to each other. Pleasing proportions are 1:2 or 2:3 and the "Golden Mean" (1:1.6). The golden mean proportion is found throughout nature, the human body, architecture, and is commonly used for commercial goods such as rugs and photo frames (3x5, 8x12).

<u>Scale</u> refers to the relative size of something compared to something else. In interior design, an adult human male is standard scale for most seating. Very large features, such as in many cathedrals and temples are meant to inspire awe but also can make us feel small. Very large furniture that looks just right in a showroom is often out of scale in our smaller rooms at home. In a child's room, furnishings

that are smaller than average size are appropriate, but in other rooms many small-scale items can feel cluttered or even childlike.

Scale can be understood from two perspectives: how one element relates to other elements in a grouping and the width of something compared to the width of something else, such as art hung over a sofa. Use the preferred proportions above. For example, art about 2/3 the width of the sofa is usually in good scale.

Rhythm is the repetition of something in a regular and/or repeating pattern, i.e., light, color, shape, etc. Just as in music, rhythm is a recurring "beat" with a bit of variation for interest.

Harmony is created when everything seems to belong, usually tied together with a common characteristic such as color or shape.

The above photos display harmony and rhythm with color and shape repeated around the rooms.

Lines and Shapes

Did you know how your eyes move along a line affects you emotionally? The marketing industry and consumer science specialists certainly do! Marketing professionals have long used the power of lines and shapes to influence *how they want us to feel* about their brand and the products they want us to buy. We can consciously use the emotional cues of lines and shapes to support our personal needs and goals when decorating and designing our homes, too.

Vertical lines convey dignity and are a frequent element in more formal design. As our eyes are lifted, feelings tend also to be elevated. For example, vertical lines are often used to inspire awe in temples and grand buildings, such as the White House.

Horizontal lines convey security, stability, and tend to be restful. Something horizontal cannot fall down. They lead the eye across something, so horizontal lines emphasize width.

Diagonal lines are all about movement and visual excitement. They are attention grabbing and hint at danger (unstable, something in motion).

Straight lines are orderly, logical, appeal to the "rational" (conscious) mind, although vertical and horizontal lines trigger very different emotional responses.

Curved lines give a sense of both freedom and comfort verses the efficiency of a straight line. They are more organic (found in nature), and suggest flow. Small curved lines tend to be playful.

Angular lines create visual interruptions and grab our interest. Like diagonal lines, angular lines are about change. Designs without curves may seem artistic and "edgy" but also can sometimes seem cutting, without much emotional warmth.

These are building exteriors, but the same principles also work for our décor choices inside our homes. Vertical lines in building design (left) tend to be formal while more horizontal lines (center) are experienced as stable and more restful. Angles (right) are often used for dramatic, artistic expression, such as in this award-winning home by Nicholas Tye Architects and local firm, John Doak Architects.

Lines combine to form shapes. Shapes trigger emotional effects similar to lines.

Squares are solid and stable; too many can feel almost rigid, boring or "boxed in."

Circles are self-contained and can feel static, not going anywhere. Round dining tables are equally inclusive. "Round table discussions" are intended to give no one person more importance than any other.

Triangles are energetic, full of visual movement with a point to which the eye is drawn.

Rectangles are also stable but more visually interesting than squares. Rectangles may have either a vertical or horizontal influence.

Ovals, like rectangles and triangles, keep the eye moving so they hold our attention longer. More eye movement makes them more dynamic than squares or circles.

"We shape our buildings and afterward our buildings shape us."

- Winston Churchill

Innergized Tips

- When choosing furnishings for your room, first consider the desired function of the space. What activities and mood do you want – relaxing and introspective, or active and energized? Then select the shapes of your furnishings that best contribute to that feeling.
- Texture and pattern are underappreciated ways of bringing dimension and interest to your spaces. Think beyond accessories. Your walls and floors are literally two of the biggest opportunities you have to bring in more texture and pattern into your rooms.
- Drapery panels soften the hard lines and sharp right angular shapes of most windows.
- At a circular table, no one is given more importance or more "voice" than another, so circular tables are great for families with challenging dynamics.
- When considering shapes in your home, include everything: the furniture, the objects within the room; the architectural features; and even the spaces between and around the furniture.
- When using textures and patterns, especially in a small space, good proportion is in the general ratio of 2:1. For example, generously use two small scale patterns or textures with one bold one used half as often for variety and pop. Either too much or too little variation can be tiring. Always include some solids to give the eyes a place to relax.

Smell and Taste

Smell has been a maligned sense in our Western culture. Our thoughts about smells in our homes have centered on odors that are considered "bad" and what to do about them. The popularity of aromatherapy is helping to change that narrow perception. Aromatherapy uses aromatic plant oils and materials for improving psychological or physical well-being - a part of wellness and spiritual traditions worldwide dating back before written records. Today, most of us still largely misunderstand and underappreciate how smells affect us within our homes.

What the Nose Knows

Scientists report that we each have a unique personal scent that instantly tells others a great deal about us and is as individual as our fingerprints. Our homes have a similar unique smell. You know that smell you immediately recognize when you walk into a friend or family member's home? This phenomenon is called "Occupant Odor." We are rarely aware of that odor in our own homes.

With scents, whatever is new in the environment is what grabs our conscious attention. If you are curious about how your house smells to a guest, pay attention when you walk back in for the first time after you've been away for a few days. The first few whiffs when we enter an area are all we have to identify ongoing smells in that space.

This may seem odd but makes sense from an evolutionary perspective. With every breath, we literally absorb tiny bits of what is around us and has been released into the air. Our noses are exquisitely sensitive to the smallest changes of these airborne molecules. This gives us an enormous amount of information almost instantly. If no danger is perceived, our bodies simply stop signaling us to be aware of those particular odors. This allows us to quickly detect and react to even the subtlest change in our environment and many odors are associated with danger. Examples include mold, gas leaks, the bacteria of decomposing food, toxic volatile organic compounds (VOCs), and smoke.

With our olfactory process, with every breath we experience almost instant shifts in mood, mental alertness, and sometimes physical reactions including healing or damage at a cellular level. Even more than with other senses, this happens outside of awareness. And there is more.

The olfactory bulb is part of the limbic system, the emotional memory part of the brain. This makes smell the most direct (fastest!) route to our emotions. A smell can trigger a flood of memories which trigger neurochemicals that influence our moods and affect our mental acuity and work performance. Research indicates that odors and emotional memory are so closely intertwined that scents influence about 75 percent of our daily emotions and play a key role in long term memory. Maybe this is part of the comfort in "comfort food" and why smells are so evocative of particular people, places and events in our lives, for better or worse. [22]

Scent-Scapes for Home

For many of us, having a clean-smelling house is important for entertaining guests. We seem to have associated the smell of a clean house with a "clean," respectable lifestyle. Consumer research indicates that for our house to really seem clean we want it to smell like a cleaning product. A couple of studies even indicate that a clean-smelling house may make us actually behave better, including being more generous and fair. [23.]

Capitalizing on this, everything seems to be chemically scented today, from garbage bags to cleaning products, to candles and more. Many commercial "air fresheners" like scented candles, incense, decorative accessories and cleaning products actually make indoor air quality worse and do nothing to reduce unpleasant odors; they simply mask the odors. Such "air fresheners" often contain toxic ingredients like phthalates, artificial fragrance, and polycystic aromatic hydrocarbons that are linked to cancer, hormone disruption, neurotoxicity, and respiratory irritation.

With a little awareness and very little effort, we can make a big impact toward healthier homes within the "scent-scapes" of our homes. You can find dozens of therapeutic-grade aromatherapy oils available in health food stores and online; many more also contain less expensive synthetic ingredients. Synthetic fragrances don't have the healing aspects of natural oils. Look for the pure oils if you want the healing power of scents and to limit toxic chemicals in your home.

Here are some commonly available essential oils with their recognized effects which have been identified in the research and are beneficial in our daily spaces:
    Energizing: ginger, rosemary, peppermint, cinnamon, citrus
    Comforting: chamomile, lavender, sandalwood, rosemary
    Focus, Memory: basil, lemongrass, peppermint, citrus
    Sleep, Relaxation: lavender, sandalwood, chamomile, rose otto
    Meditation: lavender, sandalwood, frankincense, cedar

There are many easy, inexpensive ways to make your home smell amazing that don't include toxic chemicals. Here are some of my favorites:

1. Deodorize. An online search will yield countless remedies for smelly kitchen drains, disposals, and other sometimes problematic areas. Vinegar and/or baking soda are both well known for their deodorizing powers. One easy triple action recipe is: Freeze vinegar in an ice-cube tray. Turn on the disposal and toss in the frozen cubes. The ice helps whisk away bits of trapped food and the vinegar kills the mold, germs, and bacteria actually responsible for the unpleasant odors. For a burst of fresh-smelling scent, include bits of lemon, orange, or other citrus either when you freeze the ice cubes or when you toss the cubes in the disposal. If a smell still persists, pour one-half cup of baking soda down the drain while running warm water.

   Charcoal is also an effective nontoxic deodorizer. You can get charcoal tablets or small bricks in pet stores or online. Just put the charcoal in a small bowel and let the deodorizing begin!

2. <u>Infuse.</u> Essential oils and aromatherapy diffusers can be purchased almost anywhere, from online to health food stores to department stores like Target and Walmart.

   - Many essential oils have antibacterial, antifungal, and antiviral properties, too. Diffusing can help not just freshen the air, but purify it as well. Simply boil a pot of water, take it off the heat, and add a few drops of essential oil, such as lemon or eucalyptus. The scent of the oils will infuse the whole room.

   - Here is an easy recipe for making your own home deodorizing spray. All you need is one tablespoon baking soda, two to three drops of your favorite essential oil (Lavender, lemon, orange, cinnamon, and peppermint are often favorites.), and some distilled water. Mix the baking soda and essential oil, then add it to a spray bottle along with the distilled water. Shake well, and it's ready to use.

   - With the following technique, you can vary the scent with the seasons or your mood without purchasing anything extra: Just simmer water in a small saucepan then add aromatic food such as citrus and/or cranberries, and your favorite herbs or spices.

3. <u>Houseplants.</u> Many houseplants are great air fresheners, cleaning the air of specific toxins. Include a kitchen herb garden or fragrant houseplants for scent-sational air as well. Here are some of my favorite easy-to-grow aromatic plants: scented geraniums, jasmine, orange jessamine, mint, sweet bay, and rosemary. For more on plants, see the plants section in chapter 7 and Plant Power in the back of the book.

Innergized Tips

- You can be subtle when adding scents to your home. Our sense of smell is powerfully responsive to even a few molecules in the air.
- Change scents to support natural rhythms. For example, include relaxing scents at the end of the day, or use an energizing perk for a midafternoon slump. You can also change with the seasons, using warming scents like cinnamon in cooler months and cooling scents like mint or citrus in the heat of summer.
- Two no-cost, minimal-effort ways to freshen the air in your home are: (1) Mist the room with a spray bottle of water; (2) open the windows. Even a few minutes a day will allow for an exchange of air and do wonders to improve indoor air quality.
- Ask that new upholstered pieces, carpeting, and other textiles be aired outdoors before they are installed in your home. If that cannot be arranged, turn the thermostat up and leave home for a couple of days. When you return, open all the windows and thoroughly air out of your home the chemicals that have out-gassed.
- If you suspect that something you smell in your home is making you sick, seek the services of a professional home inspector or specialist in that particular area. Some serious indoor air problems such as carbon monoxide and radon have no odor at all. The International Institute for Building Biology & Ecology (IBE.com) and the Healthy Building Environmental Learning Center (hbelc.org) are good resources for more information and certified specialists.
- Use essential oils instead of commercial air fresheners and deodorizers. Essential oils are non-toxic and many, like lavender and peppermint, have antiviral, antibacterial, and antifungal properties. Essential oils smell great while they sanitize and disinfect.
- Check online and in your library for aromatherapy books to explore other scents and their amazing effects.

Taste

Taste is closely associated with smell. Freshly baked cookies or bread create wonderful aromas, and the anticipation of enjoying the taste is an essential part of the experience. Including the smell of freshly baked cookies or bread has become a cliché staging technique for evoking feel-good emotions when a home is for sale. A platter of cookies on the table to be shared is a bonus in that experience.

Food is essential to our health at the most fundamental level. We feed our young and share collectively what has been gathered. All cultures have some form of food-sharing customs and rituals. The phrase "breaking bread" with someone implies a sense of brotherhood or partnership, a meaningful connection between people or a group, with or without food. To "break bread" may be one of our oldest human traditions, dating back to prehistory.

For our purposes of interior design, the sense of taste has little direct application except perhaps as a metaphor for your decorating preferences. In holistic interior design, it is your personal "taste" that matters, not the "tastemakers" du jour.

However, you can encourage healthier eating, wonderful memories, and positive social interaction through your design and décor choices which are explored in the kitchen and dining portion of chapter 8.

Sound

Sound is probably so overlooked in traditional interior design because it cannot be seen or touched. But sound touches us emotionally and physically. Sound is a form of energy produced by vibration. Our responses to sound are highly individual in both our waking and sleeping lives. Sound has been used to evoke moods, activities, healing, and spiritual interaction for eons, but we now know more about why sound is so effective at these things.

Only very recently scientists learned how sounds are linked to emotional centers in the brain. Like sight and smell, sound is connected to memory and emotion, which quickly trigger positive or negative reactions. Sounds also affect us physically, with cellular transformations affecting blood circulation, the nervous system, metabolism, and the endocrine glands in a positive *or* negative way. Maybe this is not new information at all, since the word "noise" derives from the Latin word for nausea.[24] So, sounds do have a great deal to do with our enjoyment or lack of enjoyment of our indoor spaces, as well as with our emotional and physical health. This knowledge can help us better include sound in our home designs for a better quality of life.[25]

Noise pollution

Noise pollution that bombards us in today's world has been extensively studied and written about. The World Health Organization (WHO), Centers for Disease Control (CDC), and researchers worldwide have been warning us about the dangerous effects of noise pollution for decades. Although often minimized as more of a nuisance than a serious quality-of-life issue, noise pollution is now increasingly recognized as a public health concern. Like air pollution, scientists are finding that even small amounts of chronic noise pollution can contribute to damaging, even deadly effects.[25, 26]

Health Effects of Noise Pollution

- Irreversible hearing loss
- Reduced cognitive abilities including concentration, productivity, and creativity
- Learning difficulties and delayed development for children
- Increased general stress levels and aggravated stress related conditions such as high blood pressure, ulcers, and migraine headaches
- General reduction in perceived quality of life and reduced opportunities for relaxation
- Increase in depression, irritability, mood swings, and even suicide
- Damage to liver, brain, and heart including increased number of deaths from cardiovascular disease

Experts believe that, except for volume that causes hearing loss, many negative reactions to noise involve lack of control and expectation as much as the increased ongoing auditory clutter in our modern world. Again, this makes sense from an evolutionary perspective. Early man would need to be able to respond to sudden or unusual noises that could indicate danger.

Today, we still react to loud unexpected noise with involuntary stress responses. Loud and unexpected sounds trigger elevated heart rates and an immediate flood of stress hormones like adrenalin. Franklin Institute research on stress and the adrenal glands reveals that even low-level chronic noise increases aggression, decreases cooperation, and is associated with increased risk for such serious problems as peptic ulcers, high blood pressure, cardiovascular diseases. [27]

In urban areas, modes of transportation (trains, planes, vehicles) generate a great deal of noise pollution. The mechanical systems and appliances inside our homes generate a great deal of noise, too. For example, a vacuum cleaner creates the noise level of about 80 decibels, the level that starts to damage your hearing if you are exposed for too long. This can be compared to average conversation levels of around 60 decibels. [27]

Sound ABCs

Improve your home acoustics with these Sound ABCs:

Absorb - Add textiles such as rugs, pillows, window treatments, and other materials with texture such as plants to absorb sound.

Block - Sound waves can be redirected with such things as sliding walls, screens, double glazed windows, and large plants.

Cover up - Providing background sound can mask intrusive sounds. Music can be effectively used for this. Sound machines often use other sounds to create an envelope of sounds that you can control in duration and volume to cover up irritating noises.

Much research and many published techniques for sound management involves sound masking (C in the above ABCs.) in business settings. Those findings have implications for us at home, too, even if we don't work from a home office. Two examples are:

- Improvement is noted in recall, creativity, and in the ability to concentrate.
- Enhanced positive emotions/comfort levels are also recorded.

Sound masking has been extensively used for enhanced sleep. Maybe it seems counterintuitive to add more sound when noise is the problem. Experts believe it is not necessarily the volume of a sound that wakes you, keeps you awake, or keeps you from concentrating. A startle response can be set off by an unexpected sound at night, for example, and wake you even when you've been soundly asleep. Evidently, sound masking works because specific sounds can blend intrusive sounds such as barking dogs, traffic, or a neighbor's television, into general background noise so your brain pays less attention.

Research findings have spawned a whole industry of sound machines. Sound machines can be a good investment for either introducing soothing sounds or for masking irritating noises. To try various sounds for the masking technique without buying a machine, a Smartphone app may be the easiest way to experiment with sounds to help you sleep, concentrate on the task at hand, or to feel calmer and more comfortable. You can find countless apps, both free and paid. But be aware that some apps use low quality sounds that you may find irritating rather than soothing, plus many experts caution that phones, computers and other blue light screens should be kept out of the bedroom for the best sleep. You can read more about this in lighting, chapter 4.

Many sound machines offer nature sounds and a variety of "color" selections for better sleep or better concentration. These machines come in a range of shapes, sizes, and costs, from high-tech expensive sound systems that vary the sonic patterns based on the acoustic makeup of the room to some low-tech affordable options. Some machines are portable and can easily move from room to room, or be taken along to calm a fussy baby in the car, or with you to a hospital room or for masking hotel noise when you travel.

The Colors of Noise

You've probably heard of white noise, but other colors of noise are getting a lot of attention these days as potential boosters for everything from better sleep, enhanced concentration and creative thinking, to health/healing and relaxation. The name white noise was selected to indicate a balanced sound frequency profile similar to white light's balanced color spectrum. Other color names, like *pink*, *red*, and *blue* were then given to noise with other spectral profiles similar to bands of light. The other sonic colors have more energy concentrated at either the high or low end of the sound spectrum, which changes the nature of the vibration. And yes, the color black is associated with silence.[28, 29]

White noise gives equal intensity to all frequencies of sound, but white noise sounds much harsher than what we would expect from a spectrally flat noise. This is because our hearing process doesn't sense all frequencies equally. Unlike white noise, pink noise creates a balance of high and low frequency sounds that mimic many sounds found in nature. People often find that more pleasant than white noise. A number of studies have shown that people exposed to pink noise during sleep spend more time in deep sleep. In a Northwestern University's Feinberg School of Medicine study, researchers found that pink noise exposure at night also led to better memory recall the next day.[30]

The everyday noises we hear, such as a car honking, shoes clattering over a floor, or jingling keys, are made up of sporadic waveforms, a random distribution of frequency and amplitude. But the inverse pattern of pink noise has been applied to systems outside of sound. An inverse pink noise pattern has been found in many genres of music, the structure of DNA, the rise and fall of the tide, the flow of traffic, and even variations in the stock market! It seems the world is basically washed in "pink" patterns that we do not see!

Positive Sound of Nature and Music

Sound machines often offer nature sounds, too. Nature sounds, especially the sounds of water, are found to be deeply relaxing, triggering responses similar to meditation responses in EKGs recording brainwaves. Nature sounds can have a restorative effect on our cognitive abilities. Studies have shown that when listening to nature sounds, workers not only performed better on task, they also reported feeling more positive and cooperative.[31]

Research presented at the Acoustical Society of America's 2015 annual meeting suggests that nature sounds may be better than white noise in boosting mood and productivity and were preferred six to one over white noise or no sounds by study participants. If you can't get out into nature or open the windows to hear the soft rustle of tree leaves in the breeze or a babbling water feature, bring the sounds of nature indoors to you! Nature sounds evidently generate a state of relaxation, contentment, and gentle focus that is mentally and physically restorative similar in EKG brain response to mediation.[31] But the specific sounds enjoyed vary individually. National Sleep Foundation experts suggest to experiment with your sound options and observe how your mind and body respond to the sounds. Breaking ocean waves might keep you alert for the next crash of water hitting land, while a steady waterfall rhythm lulls you quickly to sleep. On my sound machine, I personally love the sound of a rainstorm with distant thunder, but others in my home find that selection anything but comforting or relaxing! If a sound pattern is stimulating, raising your heart rate, filling you with energy or a strong emotional reaction, then keep searching for the soothing sounds that are right for you for relaxing sleep.

Music has been important in all cultures and has been studied extensively for its impressive psychological and physiological effects. Entire books have been dedicated to the subject. Music deserves attention beyond this brief introduction to holistic interior design. Not much will be included here except to remind you to include a variety of music in your home to help create the right mood and encourage specific activities. For example, use upbeat and faster music to help you be more productive with tedious tasks or generate a lively party atmosphere; softer music that's gently rhythmic or with steady repetition reminiscent of a heartbeat is good for relaxing and winding down in the evening, encouraging introspection, or soothing a cranky little one, like a classic lullaby. The National Sleep Foundation recommends music with rhythms between sixty- to-eighty beats per minute, often found in classical, folk, and jazz music to help you wind down.[32]

Even low-level chronic noise pollution has serious health effects and is a major health concern. However, many positive effects of specific sounds and patterns of sound include: better sleep, faster healing, pain reduction (even better than aspirin!), stress reduction, better concentration, enhanced mood and energy, and more. As with the other senses, awareness is the key to good sound management. To help get you started, a sound management activity is included in the back of the book.

Innergized Tips

- The ABCs are an easy prompt for brainstorming sound design options for your home.
- Techniques for blocking unwanted sound from outside your doors are usually energy saving, too - a double win! Consider weather stripping and double-glazed windows in this category.
- Good sound management includes and goes beyond removing irritating and distracting sounds. Good sound management includes positive ambient sounds, too. Complete silence is unnatural and not ideal either. Can you imagine your home mostly the color of black? Luckily, hearing may be one of the senses easiest to enhance at home. Besides adding music and recorded sounds you can open a window to appreciate the rustle of a breeze through the leaves and better hear the birds outside your home; a bubbling water feature is another way to bring positive, soothing sounds indoors.
- Enhance your acoustic comfort with a mix of a variety of soft textiles to absorb unwanted sound. Use a mix of upholstered furniture, pillows, rugs, and other textiles such as fabric panels at the windows, to absorb noise pollution.

Touch

Our bodies are like one big touch receptor. Maybe that is why it has been difficult to study touch apart from other senses. Our sense of touch both directly and indirectly connects us to the physical world around us. In traditional interior design, we often talk about the importance of tactile elements in our spaces, but the impact of our sense of touch is still often underappreciated and overlooked.

Touch is a very sensual and yet very practical sense. Throughout our lives, tactile sensations remain important to our physical and mental health. We need and love our creature comforts: a warm cuddly blanket, smooth cool sheets, thick fluffy towels, cushy supportive seating. Heating, cooling, and airflow are part of tactile comfort (or discomfort). Thermal consistency is not most conducive to healthy living or overall home satisfaction. Much like with sound, a sense of control and variation is needed for the most satisfactory thermal experience in any room. A cooling breeze from an open window or fan and the warmth radiating from a fireplace across our skin are part of the comfort of touch.

Texture and textiles convey emotional feelings. Even when we do not actually touch them, textures and textiles send visual impressions of physical sensations. These visual messages can sometimes be misleading, but we rely on our tactile senses including visual clues, to help us avoid danger as well as to soothe and comfort us. Soft, woven texture like flannel cotton is comforting. Hard, rough textures such as rough stone are stimulating rather than soothing, encouraging action more than rest.

Pay attention to the things that touch you at home. How well do your furnishings support your body, your activities, and your moods? How does the flooring underfoot feel? Our feet, like our hands, have thousands of nerve endings. What you walk over has profound effect on your overall perceptions of an environment. Is the flooring consistent throughout your home or is there variety? Hard surfaces like tile feel solid and secure but can signal danger of a fall if slick or uneven. Wood also feels solid but seems warmer than tile. Carpet and rugs usually add soft, cushy comfort underfoot but may be scratchy like most sisal rugs.

Research has revealed that just seeing scenes of nature stimulates a structure in the brain that seeks information through the senses, and that includes tactile visual impressions. Nature scenes with the greatest amount of variety and randomness produce the greatest amount of pleasure-linked brain activity, indicating the greatest pleasure for the viewer.[21, 31] A mirror to reflect a window view with trees or including indoor plants in your décor are simple ways of providing at pleasurable tactile stimulation visually.

Contrast and variety are important to include when choosing textures and patterns for your home.

Nature's designs include variety, randomness, and diversity, often with curvy lines moving your eyes in a flowing way. Human designs tend to be more uniform, angular, and rigid.

Touch and textures can be subtle factors that are the difference between a good-looking space that is missing an elusive something and a great space that invites you to linger and relax.

Especially when access to a window with a view is unavailable, remember that since the research indicates that it is the variation in natural patterns, textures, and colors that brings us the greatest pleasure, think of ways to create sensory variety and tactile stimulation within your home. Do you find a variety of tactile sensations in every room? Do the materials in your rooms support the moods and activities you want there, visually and physically? Is your furniture comfortable? Is the available seating varied in size and style? Here are some tactile design tips.

Innergized Tips

- Our design choices should soothe and engage, not trigger concern or anxiety. Examples of concern are sharp edges on furniture, slippery flooring, or rugs that can trip us.
- A variety of textures and textiles add a sense of fullness and complexity to any room. They help even a small space live large and help a large and cold space feel more inviting.
- A harmonious supportive home does not scream, *"Look at me!"* Too much contrast can be jarring or exhausting. However large or small the tactile patterns, they can be either bold or subtle if harmoniously connected by other lines, patterns, colors, and shapes within the visible area.
- In the name of cleanliness, bathrooms and kitchens are often full of hard, smooth surfaces. Add a variety of textures with textiles to make them more appealing.

- With today's options, shower heads can be a great source for a variety of energizing or soothing tactile stimulation in the shower.
- Ergonomics is often thought of in relationship to a working environment. Ergonomics is the field of spatial layout, equipment, and furnishings for physical comfort, safety, and productivity. Comfortable, safe, supportive furniture and spatial layouts should be for every home as well as work environments. Comfortable, truly supportive furniture is less expensive than bodies out of alignment.
- Even beyond considering personal style preferences, one shape and size chair does not fit all. Offer a variety in seating throughout your home. Dining chairs, for example, do not need to match but do need to be comfortable.
- Bring natural materials and textures from nature into your home for easy, inexpensive, and impactful home décor for your overall well-being. For example, a couple of low maintenance plants can improve your indoor air, mood, and mental functioning while their pattern and texture instantly aesthetically enhances your home.
- Walls and floors are often overlooked opportunities for added texture. Try putting a branch from your yard into a large floor vase and then use a small up-light to shine through the foliage from below for impressive textural shadows on the ceilings and walls.

Include living things and natural materials.

Flooring and thermal variations are important considerations in a room's tactile comfort.

Sensory Awareness Summary

Physical and emotional response to sensory stimulus is fast - too fast for conscious processing. Therefore we remain largely unaware of its influence. It takes our brains about a quarter of a second to identify a sensory trigger, and about another quarter of a second to produce the chemicals that are released throughout our bodies, not just in our brains. Together they form a feedback loop between our brains and bodies which has been measured by blood flow, brain activity, facial expressions, and muscular responses.[21]

We too often try to dismiss internal body signals that can help us develop self-awareness and connection to the world around us. Whatever you're doing, and whatever you are sensing, give it your full attention. Even though processed outside our awareness, with greater sensory awareness of our sensory triggers we can become more consciously connected to our world and feel more at home and whole within ourselves.

4

Power Tools: Color and Light

Color

Color and light are design power tools; they provide powerful nonverbal communication that affects us at every level of our being and instantly influences our experience of an environment.

The importance of light and color in our well-being would be difficult to overestimate.

All color is from light. Light, darkness, and the colors of the natural spectrum are energy patterns that we can see. Both color and sunlight are waves of electromagnetic energy that affect every cell in our bodies. Our biochemistry depends upon sunlight and all of its natural cycles.

Languages and everyday metaphors are rich with symbolism of color, light, and darkness. Both color and light have been used for healing and in spiritual ceremonies and rites across cultures for thousands of years and are a part of many creation stories.

Universal physical responses to colors are instinctive and biological in response but, as with all symbolism, our responses also can be heavily influenced by cultural associations and personal experiences. With travel and social media today, we are less rigid in cultural color symbolism.

Because so many of my clients and seminar participants have questions and concerns about color, we will start with color as our first power tool in the holistic design toolbox.

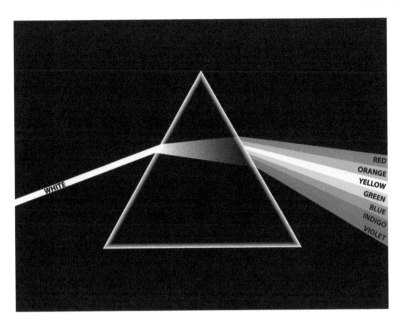

Color is a fun, nonverbal communication triggering reaction at all levels: physical, mental, and emotional. In fact, there is no way to avoid color's influence on us. Even "safe" white and beige trigger an emotional message and a physical reaction. The only way to play it safe with color is to have a good idea of the results you want when using it in a room. For example, did you realize that red speeds up heart rate, encourages social interaction, and aids in digestion? No wonder red is a traditional favorite for dining rooms and restaurants!

Color Power

Color is a power element in any room. As much as 70 percent of our <u>conscious</u> reactions to our environments may be tied to color, but our reactions depend upon many factors.[33] How we feel about a color or color combination often varies with the circumstances.

Like people, colors have general personality traits *and* physical traits. Some are warm, bold, and outgoing. Some are decidedly subdued and stay in the background. Others tend to be comforting. And, also like people, colors influence one another and will be influenced by other factors in the surrounding environment. Did you know that specific colors and color combinations can promote specific physical and emotional responses such as soothing and relaxing us, or encouraging livelier interaction, or making us feel warmer or cooler within the same temperature setting?

Complex, pervasive, and powerful, our reactions to color are partly biology and partly influenced by both cultural and personal experiences. For example, here in the West, white is often associated with purity and weddings, but it's the color of death and mourning in China. The following research is drawn heavily from our Western perspective.

Red is like a jolt of caffeine - physically stimulating - and is the most physically activating color. Red can increase blood pressure, breathing rates, social interaction, stimulate appetite, and enhance the sense of smell. Red makes us feel warmer, so rooms painted red and certain shades of pink can comfortably be set at a lower temperature.

Red stirs a full range of emotions and whatever is triggered is robust, not timid. Red has the longest wavelengths visible to the human eye and is an attention grabber that will not be ignored. The color red can support mental engagement and the attention necessary for cognitively intense tasks.

Dark reds can be elegant or glamorous while complex brown-reds have some of the grounding personality of brown. Tints of pink can be associated with innocence, femininity, gentleness or, negatively with youthful naivety without power.

Orange sparks creativity, sociability, vitality, increases energy; much like red, it is physically stimulating. Bolder shades, like a bold spice, are often best used in small amounts. Dark muted shades and light tints are more mellow and livable, even in larger amounts.

Soft pale tints of orange are flattering to most skin types, helping us look good as well as feel good. Although few people's favorite color, orange is accepted by most people. Orange, a blend of red and yellow, is associated with sociability, exotic cultures, warm climates, and affordability. Orange can be negatively associated with what is brash and/or inexpensive.

Yellow is the color the eye identifies first, so use yellow and splashes of yellow to direct attention. Yellow can warm and brighten both our physical spaces and our emotional outlooks. Yellow is said to be the color of the intellect. Bright yellow can be overpowering, much like glaring sunlight. Yellow can be negatively associated with what is dated/aged or untrustworthy.

Green is in the middle of the color spectrum and neither recedes nor advances visually. Green is the largest color family discernable to the human eye. The wide range of tones and shades triggers very different responses. With more yellow, it can be stimulating or seem unhealthy; with more blue, green is calming. Bright and deep greens are stimulating. With too much intense green we can feel unsettled.

Natural greenery in an environment or even seen in a window view is known to speed heal-ing and refresh us mentally. Often green is said to relax, but green is more a color of renewal, growth, and change.

Blue can lower blood pressure, slow down breathing, reduce appetite, physically cool us and contrib-ute to a Zen-like sense of calm. Blue is also associated with sorrow. Blue is a universally liked color, but is not always our first choice in décor.

Sky blue stimulates the pituitary gland to release calming hormones. Some blue-grays and blue-greens produce a similar effect. Darker blues add an aura of seriousness, importance, and responsibility. Many blues cool us, literally; rooms with blue walls can be comfortably set at several degrees higher temperatures.

Purple/Violet is associated with whimsy, creativity, and royalty. At the end of the visible spectrum, purple is also often linked with spirituality, the mysterious and the unseen. In Latin cultures, purple is the color of mourning. Purples are versatile, evoking a range of strong personal reac-tions. The tone and intensity greatly influence purple's message. Deep saturated purples are linked with luxury and opulence in our Western perspective.

Neutrals (not in the spectrum):

Black makes a strong visual impact. It can add sense of sophistication and mystery and help create or define clear boundaries. Black can also be experienced as challenging, foreboding, or as-sociated with what is bad. Black soaks up natural light, but with enough artificial light it can be great for drama and contrast. Black makes our eyes work hard and often is best used as an accent color.

White conveys a sense of cleanliness, purity, and coolness. Not an especially friendly color, too much white can seem cold and sterile. Contrary to popular belief, research indicates that white walls do not make rooms appear significantly larger but white walls do allow individual elements within a room to be especially noticed. Warm white offers a vintage feel, is more classic than contemporary, and is generally more approachable than a cool white.

Brown is grounding. It evokes stability, practicality, physical and emotional comfort, and warmth. Brown can be rich and sensual or unassuming and "down to Earth." This hardworking neutral has variations that will work well with most colors. Too much brown can be experienced as unimaginative and boring.

<u>Grey</u> is linked with creativity. In advertising, grey is often used for a sophisticated, conservative, or serious corporate message. Versatile grey can convey elegance or serious business, and an edgy high-tech, or vintage-industrial style. Grey also can be experienced as gloomy or drab. Most neutrals, especially the greys, have enough of another color to reflect that color's "personality" and warm or cool undertone.

Color Schemes and Palette Selection

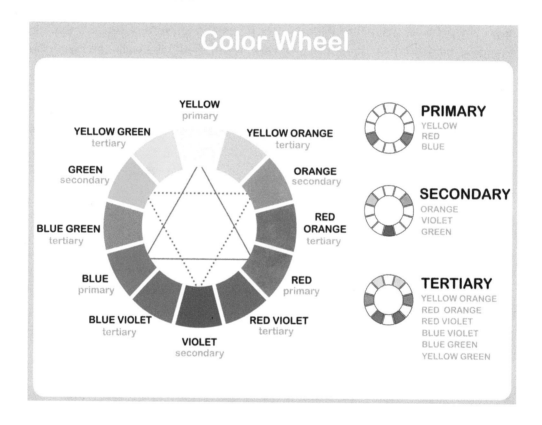

A <u>Color Wheel</u> is the visible color spectrum arranged in a circle. This is a handy, inexpensive tool for seeing natural color relationships at a glance. Here are some of those relationships:

<u>Primary Colors</u> (red, blue, and yellow in paints) cannot be made by combing other colors.

<u>Secondary Colors</u> are created by combining two primary colors. They are found half way between the primary colors combined to create them and next to the tertiary colors.

<u>Tertiary or Intermediary Colors</u> are created by combining a secondary color and a primary color next to each of them on the color wheel.

Complementary Colors are opposite one another on the color wheel, like red and green. When mixed they "neutralize" and create the many variations of brown. When complementary colors are placed side by side they seem to intensify one another. This energizing effect is why sports teams often select complementary colors for their team colors. But pairs of these colors can be too visually jarring for every day when the hue intensities are similar and used in equal amounts.

Warm Colors (red, orange, yellow) are energetic colors that appear to advance toward you.

Cool Colors are opposite on the wheel (blue, green violet) and seem to recede and encourage introspection.

Neutrals are said to be neither warm nor cool, so work well with other colors. Traditional neutrals are not found on the color wheel (white, gray, brown, black) but many colors can be toned down to be basically neutral, i.e. neither cool nor warm.

Common Color Schemes

Monochromatic: A monochromatic color scheme uses varying tints and shades of one hue. This creates a unified feeling but can be restful or even dynamic with bold variations in hue.

Analogous: This color scheme includes colors (usually three) that are side by side on the color wheel. Often a neutral or a color of the opposite temperature is added as accent and balance.

Complementary: Based on colors opposite each other on the color wheel, one color is dominant and the other is used as accent.

Triadic: A triadic color scheme uses colors at the points of an equilateral triangle. The main color and one accent color are selected from the same temperature group (warm or cool); the other accent color is from the opposite temperature group. Note the dotted line triangles within the color wheel.

Color palette selection is choosing the specific shade or tint that you will use.

Challenges of palette selection are often around undertones. Pesky undertones are usually a temperature problem. Warm woods (yellow or red tones) can set off green undertones, so pair warm woods with warm colors or with a neutral with yellow or red undertones. Unexpected pink undertones can appear when used near blue, green, or violet colors. To neutralize an unwanted pink undertone, try adding a neutral with a warm yellow undertone. With unwanted undertones, before repainting, try replacing light bulbs with the correcting warm or cool light, explored in lighting, our next power tool.

Vibrant, subdued, or monochromtic, if a color scheme works in nature it will also work for you at home. Selecting your color scheme from the natural environment around your home is a great way to find inspiration and bring the rejuvenating influence of nature indoors.

Innergized Tips

- Colors found in vegetation, fruits, flowers, and other elements associated with healthy natural landscapes are also perceived as healthy colors in an indoor living environment.
- Look for inspiration from outside your windows or from a favorite piece of art, fabric, pillow, or the most expensive, visually commanding upholstered piece (usually the sofa).
- Avoid 50/50 color scheme proportions, which feel unnatural and static. Pleasing proportions are 1:3. In a three-color palette, try 60-30-10 or 70-20-10 and include the wood tones.
- Small spaces do not mean you have to have white walls. Deeper shades can add depth and dimension, creating an inviting backdrop for belongings and activities. Mid-tones tend to enfold and unify objects in a room, making a space seem larger.
- Include neutrals in every color scheme. Remember that most neutrals, even whites, usually have enough of another color to be either warm or cool.
- Use some warm white or cream to balance bold, hot colors or to add subtle warmth to a cool room.
- Staying "on trend" is aiming for a constantly moving target. To freshen a color scheme with trendy colors, add the updated colors with accessories, which can be easily changed.
- Trim and ceiling paint do <u>not</u> have to contrast with the walls, especially if you do not want to direct attention to those features. Use contrast where and to what you want noticed.
- Contrast also can change the perceived shape and size of the space or an object. Visually enlarge a space by minimizing the boundaries. Try painting walls, ceilings, and/or trim the same or similar color, or soften visual edges by adding some of the wall paint to the white of the ceiling. Try at least one part wall pigment to 10 parts white ceiling paint. The blending of the room's elements create a more open and spacious look.

- Some paint manufacturers such as Sherwin Williams offer paint chips that include the light reflectance values (LRV). On a scale of 0 to 100, the higher the LRV number, the more reflective the color.
- Different regional areas and regional decor call for different colors and color combinations. A bright, hot tropical color scheme in New England's cooler natural light, for example, can be jarring.
- Go for blending colors not color matching. Matching is dated, unnatural, and almost impossible anyway. Texture, paint sheen, and lighting all change a color's appearance.
- Don't skimp on your paintbrushes or rollers. Good quality brushes provide smooth, full coverage without streaks or shed bristles.
- If you rent, you can still have color on your walls. Removable wallpaper can be a colorful addition or can be painted then easily removed without damage to the walls when it is time to move. Bold color combinations can be exciting in limited applications or for high-energy areas such as a home gym.
- Darker exterior colors may make a house appear smaller but more substantial. White and light exterior colors appear to advance, i.e., appear closer. Light colors on a large house may make the house look smaller but more in balance on a small lot.
- If you plan on painting, consider not just the color but also the chemicals and materials that the paint contains. Many paints contain toxic VOCs (volatile organic compounds) that are released into the air as the paint product is used. VOCs can cause health issues like dizziness, nausea, and headache. Use only low VOC or no VOC paints that won't harm you or the planet. Check the label to be certain, especially when painting rooms for infants, children, and anyone with compromised health,

Photo Examples

Here are some photo examples for using color as a power tool.

With five doorways, this space was more of an intersection than a room. Existing pale green walls (left) would never create "light and airy" so we went for a cozy and intimate destination point (right). The owner had a large living room perfect for the monthly gathering she hosted, but a cozy place for a drink and quiet conversation or cuddling with a friend to watch television or movies had been missing before the transformation.

Warm neutral colors with a variety of textures and lighting (left) bring a sense of dimension to this kitchen (before right). The warm earthy colors were carried into the adjoining rooms as seen in the following photo.

Lighting

Interior Lighting 101

Lighting does so much more than allow us to see what is in a space. Lighting not only changes how you perceive the features of a room but also how you live in it and how you feel while you are there. Although the use of natural daylight and its patterns are probably the most recognized of the biophilic design principles[7], underutilizing and misusing the power of lighting remain common in our homes.

<u>Types of Lighting</u>

1. Natural sunlight is always the best lighting source. The design technique of maximizing natural sunlight is called daylighting and may come with some design challenges such as thermal discomfort and glare control. In nature, light is diffused and varying, not evenly distributed, and never contains short blue spectral wavelengths at night.

2. Artificial Lamps (bulbs)

    Incandescent lights are the standard light bulb which hasn't changed much since Edison. Because they are such an energy hog, they are being phased out but are still available at present.

    Fluorescent lights usually emit a cool light and use much less electricity than incandescent bulbs. All fluorescents contain mercury. Although energy efficient, I cannot recommend them.

Halogen lights are brighter, last longer, and are more energy efficient than other incandescent bulbs. They can get very hot, and are close to sunlight in color temperature.

LED lights are small, very energy efficient, and can run nonstop for years. There's a wide range of LED lights on the market today. The main problem with LEDs has been the cost but they are rapidly becoming more affordable. Now there is increasing concern about health implications as they often emit a short blue wavelength without the counterbalancing healing and regenerative near-infrared frequencies needed for cellular repair and regeneration.[34]

Some LEDs are made to be more like natural sunlight in color range. One good one is Soraa Radiant 60-watt replacement LED. Another bonus with this bulb is that it is said to prevent the headaches that some LED bulbs cause by reducing the undetectable flicker effect found in LEDs.

Lighting Qualities

Diffusion — is the scattering of light rays which softens shadows and reduces glare.

Reflection — bounces light off of surfaces, including the walls and ceilings of a room. The higher the surface sheen, the greater the reflection. Polished, glassy, mirror-like surfaces have the highest light reflection.

Color — will be warm (more yellow or red) or cool (more blue in appearance) in lamps (bulbs). Natural sunlight contains both in varying amounts throughout the day and the seasons.

Watts verses Lumens

Watts refer to how much energy is used with a lamp, i.e., bulb. Lumens refer to how much visible light is produced with the lamp (bulb), the actual brightness emitted. Both are usually listed on the packaging.

Kelvin (K)

Kelvin is the color temperature of the light emitted.

There are two different kinds of color temperature: (1) Physical color temperature is the temperature of a light in degrees Kelvin (K). This applies to sunlight, candlelight, incandescent lamp light, and halogens which all emit heat. The light source itself is as hot to the touch as the color temperature given (K). (2) Correlated color temperature is a measurement that tells you how the light source appears to the human eye. A correlated color temperature of 2,700 K means it looks the same as a heat-generating light source with a physical temperature of 2,700 K. The higher the rating, the cooler (more blue) the appearance of the light emitted. The problem is that a light can LOOK the same as a warm, heat-producing light, and not actually have the same light wavelengths. On a cellular level your body and retina are not fooled by what your eye may perceive.

We prefer warm temperatures of around 2700 K, similar to light emitted by candlelight, firelight, and incandescent bulbs. For millennia, we were only exposed to fire light at night and our bodies are adapted to that. LEDs can go up to 6,500 K. In this case, the closer you are to the incandescent color temperature, the better.

Color Rendering Index (CRI)

Color rendering Index (CRI) is a scale from 0 to 100 percent, indicating how accurate a light source is at rendering color when compared to the sun. Sunlight has a CRI of 100 and so do incandescent light bulbs and candles. The higher the CRI, the better the color-rendering ability. Light sources with a CRI of 85 to 90 are considered good at color rendering. One way to get a healthier LED light is to look at the CRI. Look for a light that has an R9 (a full red spectrum) with CRI of about 97; this is the closest you'll ever get to sunlight with an LED.

Interior Lighting Options

Natural lighting may be available from windows, doors, and skylights. Nothing beats natural light. The direction of the light and the time of day and season change the quality of the light.

General lighting is usually overhead, ceiling-mounted lighting. Recessed pot lights are a popular source of general lighting. A torchiere floor lamp or a chandelier that lights up a large part of a room also can be your general lighting source.

Ambient lighting also is called general lighting in interior design, but can be "moody" and softer, such as created with dimmers, firelight, and candles. Combine ambient lighting with task lighting for inviting pools of light.

Task lighting can be a floor lamp or a table lamp that allows enough light to do a specific task such as reading, computer work, etc. Task lighting can also help create a specific mood.

Accent lighting highlights something such as artwork, a piece of furniture or architectural feature, or may "wash" a focal wall. Accent lighting is directional and adds a layer or layers of dimension to a room.

Backlighting comes from behind a subject. Backlighting is a common living room lighting error, putting people's faces in shadow.

Cove lighting is a form of indirect lighting built into ledges and recesses in a ceiling or high on the walls of a room. It directs light up towards the ceiling and down adjacent walls. This versatile technique can be used aesthetically for the lighting effect alone or used to highlight an architectural feature.

Spotlights may be uplights or downlights, and are designed to guide the eye toward an area or a particular item. Uplights especially create wonderful textural interest by casting shadows and can visually raise the height of the ceiling.

Common Types of Lighting	Design Benefit of Each
Overhead	
Whole Ceiling Lighting	is obvious overall lighting intended to provide even lighting; recessed lighting in this category can sometimes be directed, as discussed in the spotlights.
Recessed Spotlights	can be pointed in different directions and are good to highlight areas such as pathways and create pools of light.
Track Lighting	offers variations of shadow and light and can usually be directed to specific areas.
Eyeball Spotlights	direct lighting for emphasis i.e., artwork or to wash a wall.
Wall	
Single Sconce	adds texture and dimension in an area

Swing Arm/Down Lights	focus down on task at hand with flexible direction.
Candlelight (or Simulated)	is good for romance, mystery, or warmth.
Neon lighting	is used for drama, high interest, or fun.
Decorative/Artistic	create focus on the light source and/or what is illuminated for a sense of drama, interest, dimension, or fun.

Light Up Your Life Safely

Our bodies have adapted to very specific lighting conditions: bright yet diffused and varied sunlight throughout the day, and low-level firelight in the evening. Modern life has inverted these lighting conditions, leading to harsh, flat, uniform artificial lighting or light deficiency during the day, and ever-increasing light excesses at night.

Disregarding biological adaptations generally contributes to poor health. To correct such unnatural lighting conditions, you can: (1) Design an indoor lighting plan that varies throughout your spaces and throughout the day while minimizing glare and other sources of eyestrain. (2) Get a healthy dose of direct sunlight daily and maximize natural sunlight sources indoors. (3) Reduce the levels of light you're exposed to in the evening and restrict blue-light wavelength sources. Common sources are smartphones, laptops, tablets, and similar devices. Downloadable apps are now available to alter the blue wavelengths on many devices.

You may already know that blue-light wavelengths in the evenings reduce melatonin production, disrupting your internal clock aka circadian rhythms. Problems associated with disrupted circadian rhythms include sleeping problems, obesity, diabetes, heart disease, and neurodegenerative diseases like Alzheimer's and cancer. You also have cells in your retina that are responsible for producing melatonin in order to regenerate the retina during the night. Decreased production of melatonin in the retina can accelerate eyesight degeneration.[34]

Incandescent bulbs including halogen lights contain the biologically important near infrared wavelengths. The cool blue light emitted by most LEDs is not balanced with the full sunlight spectrum. These artificial blue wavelengths appear to always be damaging to our biology and far more so at night.[34]

For the lights you most often use at night, such as reading lamps, you want a 2,700 K incandescent, thermal light source. Use incandescent bulbs that are crystal clear and not coated with white to create a cool white light. For energy savings, LEDs are the best but limit them to the areas you spend less time, especially at night. The closest you'll ever get to a natural light with an LED is a light with a color temperature of about 2700 K, a R9 (full red spectrum) and CRI of about 97. Candles and firelight can be a healthy ambient light source to include in your lighting plan for recommended variations in lighting After all, this is the light that our ancestors used, so our bodies are adapted to it. But be selective. Many candles, both toxic paraffin and soy, contain lots of toxins such as dyes and fragrances plus other toxic chemicals and carcinogens. Some soy candles are only partially soy and include many toxins. Many candles also have lead in the wicks and burn with accompanying soot, adding dangerous particulates to the air. All contribute to indoor air pollution; however, this can be easily minimized by using only high-quality beeswax or soy with natural ingredients. Avoid candles with metal center wicks, and keep a window cracked open while the candle is burning.

Dimmers can add lighting variation of intensity for changes in the season, the weather, and desired mood or for various types of activities. However, some LED dimmer bulbs make a low buzzing noise because the electromagnetic resistance used to dim them creates noise. Dimmers also add "dirty electricity." Look for more on dirty electricity aka electromagnetic smog in chapter 5.

Visual Ergonomics

Be aware of and include visual ergonomics in your lighting choices. Visual ergonomics is a subsection of the field of ergonomics. It is concerned with the contribution of visual elements, including the impact of light and color in a setting to promote physical and mental well-being and academic accomplishment.[35] Suggestions include:

1. Minimize glare: reduce direct and indirect reflection
2. Generally minimize sharp contrasts in color and lighting.
3. Minimize visual clutter.
4. Relax eye strain and refresh cognitive functioning with visual "nature" breaks with a window view or even a view of indoor plants.

Innergized Tips

- Lighting everything uniformly is flat, unnatural, and means high-lighting nothing at all. Research shows that social interaction, mood, and even productivity can be dampened with uniform lighting.
- Use several lighting sources to vary intensity, levels, and direction of lighting. Your rooms immediately seem more comfortable and interesting and even feel larger. Include both table and floor lamps, some with down-light and some with up-light. If you use an overhead fixture, try to vary the light direction and consider using a dimmer.
- Add lighting to anything or any area that you want people to notice or be drawn toward.

- Most table lamps and floor lamps focus the light downward, perfect for tasks. Small pools of light also encourage conversation and small group interactions.
- Replace florescent lighting. Better, healthier options for the Earth and you are available.
- Wall sconces can direct attention, highlight something near, or provide a layer of light in the upper reaches of a room. If there is no wiring or you are concerned with the safety of candles, consider using battery-operated candles with a remote.
- Natural daylight is the best lighting. But too much of this good thing can result in glare or eye-strain and thermal discomfort along with higher utility bills, and damaged furnishings from UV rays. These challenges can be addressed with appropriate window coverings. For specifics see Special Considerations and Room By Room for window covering tips.
- To avoid glare from bulbs, lamps should be positioned so the bottom edge of the lampshade is at or just below ear or cheek level.
- Use different sources and layers of lighting, ideally from three sides of a room. At least one source should focus on something within the room, like art or architectural detail.
- When using different light sources in a room, variations of color temperature will probably be obvious. Check lamps (bulbs) as a group for harmonious color temperature.
- Check samples of fabric and furnishings in the changing light of your own home. The quality of the lighting in your home will be different in the store and will affect the perceived color of fabric, wood tones, etc. This is known as metamerism and sometimes seems almost inevitable. These surprises are connected to undertones and lighting color temperatures, which can change even with natural light throughout the day.
- Light fixtures can also be art. Add interest to a neutral background or in a small space by using fun as well as functional lamps or fixtures.
- To increase the amount of natural daylight in a room, consider adding a skylight, solar tubes, glass door panels, or a greenhouse window.
- Over-illumination at night is a needless drain on your budget and your health. The rhythm of light and dark is what drives our circadian clock, Use lower levels of light throughout the evening and sleep in a bedroom that is as dark as possible.
- Websites such as www.Houzz.com offer articles on home lighting including how-to guides, general lighting design, and shopping tips. Specialty publications for lighting are other good resources. Use guidelines as just that, a guide, then adjust to your own needs.

Photo Examples

Get creative in tight spaces. This client traveled a great deal, resulting in erratic sleeping schedules. Blackout window panels (right) completely block the light for better sleep. In such tight spaces, consider wall mounted lamps (left). The floor lamp serves as art, too (right).

Multiple sources of lights are needed to "zone" large rooms for different activities. The larger the space, the more you need lighting to create smaller, more intimate activity areas.

Brilliant Lighting

Juliette Byrne Limited

Above left, lighting is distributed around the room with table lamps, indirect accent lighting, natural light from the window, and potential firelight from the fireplace and candles on the coffee table. A mirror also reflects the light, appearing to increase the available light. Above right, layers of lighting add invitation, interest, and dimension in a hallway.

Under the Radar: Symbolism and Other Clues, Cues, and Triggers

At least 95 percent of what guides our thoughts, feelings, and actions is outside of our conscious awareness, according to neuroscience.[36,37] These "under the radar" processes include sensory stimulation, symbolic associations and impressions formed in childhood - all no doubt helping us survive as a species and still shaping our experiences today. Many of us have read and debated the implications of these findings but have overlooked their impact in our home-design choices.

An average of two-thirds of our lives are spent at home.[1] Physical settings deeply impact the people within those settings on many levels. Social scientist Roger Barker's ground-breaking 1960s studies indicated that a physical setting is more predictive of children's behavior than basic personality traits. Barker's studies on physical settings and children's behaviors were instrumental in creating the more holistic, interdisciplinary emphasis in environmental psychology studies of today.

Some of our perceptions are hard wired as universally shared reactions of biological beings and some are very individual. Our individual reactions are very influenced by experience-based emotions. With greater awareness of our reactions, we can change how we interact with and within our spaces, literally changing what is experienced on a daily basis.

Life Is Not a 2-D Experience

Life is not a 2-D experience like seeing a photo. Looking at or into a room is a very different experience than being in that space. Regardless of how you respond to the bold contrasts of the energizing office on the next page, working within this room would be a very different sensory experience than looking at this photo. Can you imagine working here? What views and unseen sensory triggers can you imagine if sitting in the chair behind the desk?

David Lauer Photography

Erin Iba Design Associates

Design for the full experience of being human.

A Sea of Interactive Energy

Western science and contemporary lifestyles have given us new energy influencers along with greater understanding of some of the ancient knowledge.[8] Science teaches us that we do not live in a universe made up of discrete physical objects (matter) separated by dead space, even if it appears to be that way. Instead, our universe is an integrated network of interactive and interdependent energy fields.

Since we do not see our physical world as interactive energy fields, here are three energy principles to remember to help design uplifting homes.

(1) Everything in our world is composed of patterns of energy including our internal physical, cognitive, and emotional responses to what is around us. The human body's biochemical and bioenergetic feedback loops are at the root of all our thoughts, emotions, and behaviors. It is not so much that we live in a sea of energy but that we are intrinsically part of that sea. Everything is connected.[36, 37]

(2) Energy constantly changes. While change is inevitable, personal growth is a choice that can be supported or challenged with our environments. While nothing stays the same, your home can be an ongoing ally for you to support your changing needs. Uplifting experiences within

our homes are essential to our quality of life individually and collectively. Positive or limiting effects can ripple out into our communities and our shared home, Earth. A healthy Earth is important to our survival as a species.

(3) Humans are bioelectrical beings. Every cell in our bodies is bathed in an external and internal environment of fluctuating electromagnetic forces. Research indicates that electromagnetic field fluctuations, both natural and man-made, can affect virtually every circuit in our biological systems.[38] We live in an unprecedented twenty-first century soup of manmade electromagnetic fields. It's not only chemicals that can create toxic environments in your home.

Electromagnetic Fields (EMFs)

According to the National Institute of Environmental Health Sciences, electromagnetic fields (EMFs) are "invisible areas of energy, often referred to as radiation, that are associated with the use of electrical power."[38]

The World Health Organization (WHO) explains that electric fields are created by differences in voltage and magnetic fields when electric current flows.[39] EMF energies include microwaves, radio waves, infrared, ultraviolet, and the visible light spectrum. WHO further explains that since our bodies have their own electric and biochemical responses, e.g., nervous system, digestion, brain, and heart functions, exposure to EMFs can interact with the human body. The electromagnetic spectrum affects every aspect of biological regulation although low-frequency and high-frequency electromagnetic waves affect the human body in different ways.

It is controversial if the amount of EMFs and related electromagnetic smog (also called dirty electricity) common in our homes can harm our health. However, with the accumulating worldwide concern, it seems likely to at least contribute to adverse health effects. It also seems probable that some of us are more sensitive to their effects than others. It seems sensible for us all to be aware of the potential dangers and the options.

You may have already heard that electromagnetic fields (EMFs) may contribute to cancer, insomnia, headaches, fatigue, and more, but what can you do to protect yourself at home?[40, 41]

- A lower EMF exposure is especially important at night when your body is doing most of its healing. This is why the bedroom is a great place to start. EMF fields weaken with distance from the source, so keep electronics out of the bedroom. If you have a choice of where to locate your home office, choose to have it as far from your bedroom as possible. Use a battery-operated alarm clock instead of an electric one or your cell phone as an alarm. In fact, store your cell phone away from your head while you are sleeping.

- Switching from wireless to hardwired devices may be the most effective way to neutralize much exposure in the home but this is not always practical. Try grounding aka Earthing.[42, 43] Emerging research has revealed that direct physical contact with the surface of the planet generates a kind of electric connection with surprisingly effective and rapid anti-inflammatory and antioxidant effects. This is significant for remaining healthy because biomedicine has discovered that many of the most debilitating diseases, and even the aging process itself, are linked with chronic inflammation and oxidative stress.[44]

- The simplest way to be grounded is to go outside and walk barefoot on the grass, sand, or dirt (preferably damp) or to immerse yourself in a body of conductive water such as water with sea salt or a mineral-rich lake.[42, 43] If indoors, a connection still can be made to the earth. The majority of domestic electrical systems offer an earth ground on every three-pronged electrical outlet. A variety of products have been developed, such as sheets, mats, bands, and patches or make them yourself with instructions in Clinton Obr's book, *Earthing*.[45]

- There are a range of EMF protection strategies and products on the market. Use due diligence in your research before you go for the EMF protection products that seem right for you.

- For further reading and research reports, Amazon.com has many highly rated books and related resources such as the DVD, *Generation Zapped*. For free resources in addition to your local library, visit online resources such as www.earthinginstitute.net, www.buildingbiology. com, and www. Mercola.com.

Negative Ions

One theory of why grounding works is that direct contact with the earth or mineral-rich water allows for an increase in negative ions to be absorbed by our bodies. Ions are odorless, tasteless, invisible, charged particles; some are charged negatively and some are charged positively. In overly simplified non-scientific terms, negative ions can be thought of as oxygen ions with an extra electron attached, produced through water molecules. This is why they are so abundant near flowing water such as rivers, streams, seas, and waterfalls. This also explains why a bath or shower can be so refreshing when we are feeling tired. We inhale these molecules in abundance in certain natural environments such as forests, mountains, waterfalls, and beaches but negative ions are found in limited number in the dry air of our homes. For example, the air around waterfalls can contain anywhere from 30,000 to 100,000 negative ions per cubic centimeter, while indoor air can contain zero to, at most, a few hundred per cubic centimeter.[46]

The benefits of negative air ionization have been validated in many studies since the mid-1980s. Negative ionization is a mild physiological stimulant. Once they reach our bloodstream, negative ions are believed to produce mild biochemical reactions that increase levels of serotonin, which helps to alleviate depression, relieves stress, and boosts our daytime energy. [47] And that's not all. Negative ions are also natural air purifiers.[48]

Dr. Albert P. Krueger, a microbiologist and experimental pathologist at the University of California, found that even a small amount of negative ions can kill bacteria quickly, reducing the chance of infection. Dr. Igho Hart Kornblueh, from the University of Pennsylvania, found that negative ions have a healing and a pain-relieving effect. In many European hospitals and workplaces, negative ionization of the air is mandatory.

WebMD estimates that one in three of us are especially sensitive to the beneficial effects of negative ions.[47] In addition, adverse reactions to positive ions can be heightened when our immune systems are already compromised. "Generally speaking, negative ions increase the flow of oxygen to the brain, resulting in higher alertness, decreased drowsiness, and more mental energy," says Pierce J. Howard, PhD, author of *The Owner's Manual for the Brain: Everyday Applications from Mind Brain Research* and director of research at the Center for Applied Cognitive Sciences in Charlotte, North Carolina. So how can you increase negative ions in your home designs?

Innergized Tips

- Add an indoor water fountain.
- Use natural fibers such as cottons, linens, bamboos, and wools instead of plastic, polyester, and chemically treated woods. Synthetic materials increase positive ions and static electricity.
- Crystal salt lamps are beautiful and often sold as negative ionizers but research indicates little negative ion increase. Since people do report enhanced well-being with their use, perhaps these beautiful lamps help in ways we do not yet understand.
- Central heating and air conditioning strip the air of humidity and negative ions. Combat dry air naturally by keeping live plants near where you spend a lot of time, including where you sleep. All plants release some water vapor into the air through their leaves in a process called transpiration. The areca and bamboo palms, and the more difficult to maintain ferns are among plants which excel at this according to NASA-based research in *How to Grow Fresh Air.*[56] For more information, see Plant Power in the back of the book.
- Nix the ashtrays! Cigarette smoke reduces negative ions in the air as well as being toxic in other ways. Never allow smoking in your home. In fact, think twice before lighting a match to anything to avoid smoke particulates in the air.
- To bring negative ionization in the indoor air to the level of a natural setting, consider one of the numerous commercial air ionizers on the market. Just avoid the "air purifying" ones that increase levels of ozone as a byproduct. Carefully check the labels.
- Spend time outdoors, especially along a green belt or running water. If this is impossible, at least open a window for the proverbial "breath of fresh air." It may be enough to help with headaches and the sense of lethargy linked to dry indoor air and the low indoor levels of negative ions.

Emotional Connections

Much has been written over the past few years about the astonishing power of our emotions. We are emotionally and biologically hardwired to respond to other people and to the physical world around us. But many of us still overlook the emotional connections found within our homes where we spend the majority of our time.

Scientists now can explain what we intuitively knew all along: when there is a difference between our thoughts and our feelings, our emotions override our thoughts every time. It is how we are wired. The emotional center's neural connections that send information to the brain's thinking centers are far more numerous and stronger than those that send information from the thinking to the emotional centers.[37] The comparatively limited influence from the cognitive system on emotional processing helps explain why it is so difficult to change habits through willpower or thoughts alone.[37] The emerging neuroscience perspective summarizes that our perceptual and emotional experiences are a composite of stimuli the brain receives from the external environment *and* internal sensations, such as thoughts and emotions.[37]

Everything in our environment, including each of our design choices, constantly sends messages to our emotional centers. These messages then trigger a variety of physical, cognitive, and emotional responses. For example, when we find a space relaxing and pleasant our bodies release calming neurotransmitters, such as serotonin and dopamine which allow us to relax more deeply. Research has even found that some design strategies that reconnect us with nature can trigger brain wave activity similar to the deep relaxation of meditation.[31] However, if a space is unpleasant, such as loud, chaotic, or with sensory cues that trigger something like eye strain or sad memories, we secrete the "flight or fight" neurotransmitter, adrenaline, or the "stress hormone," cortisol. These neurotransmitters make us even more on edge and anxious, increasing blood pressure, muscle strain, and other physical stress indicators.

Design your home to be an active ally in minimizing challenging emotions and stress. You then can achieve a greater sense of connectedness, balance, and physical, emotional and psychosocial well-being with less effort. Many responses to design choices occur together. For example, reducing a physical health challenge such as air pollution by using more natural materials that do not off-gas is likely to also improve mood and decrease stress levels as you physically feel better.

Researchers have found that emotional awareness can be heightened and is important in developing higher levels of human interactions. Emotional awareness involves an integration process of both external information and internal body signals that strengthens "whole person" development. We become more capable of identifying and addressing problems at all levels within and beyond our doors.

To override our preprogrammed subconscious emotional responses and eliminate energy-draining, stressful triggers requires more than positive thinking and willpower. Design changes that stack the deck in your favor, alter the brain's pathways, as well as the neurochemicals and electrical brain wave oscillations. Then, instead of being a source of additional irritation and stress, our homes become partners in creating life-enhancing experiences on a daily basis.

A Pattern Seeking Dynamic Duo: The Conscious and The Unconscious

The conscious and subconscious parts of being human are a pattern-seeking dynamic duo, intrinsically linked. The subconscious acts like a powerful programmable computer database of instincts and stored memories and can be very literal. The conscious mind is more like the creative voice of our thoughts. It is what allows us to speculate on possibilities, plan, and dream up innovative ideas. While we are consciously busy with creative ideas, daydreams, plans, and possibilities, the subconscious controls most everything else that we need to do to function.

For efficiency, our subconscious rapidly categorizes all stimuli into patterns. Our attention always is grabbed by changes in environmental patterns. The Free Dictionary summarizes the influence of patterns this way: "Person and environment are defined as co-extensive, open energy fields. The two evolve together and move toward increasing complexity and diversity, manifested in patterns of interaction. An understanding of *pattern* is basic to an understanding of health or holistic design, and involves the movement from looking at parts to looking at the whole. Pattern is defined as information that depicts the whole, and gives an understanding of the meaning of relationships. Natural systems as wholes, are synergistic and more than a sum of their parts."[49]

For eons, we have used natural materials, energy patterns, and abstract symbols to tell our stories and relate to the world around us.

Symbolism

Symbols are another form of patterns to which our minds and bodies quickly respond. Symbols associate one thing, often a common object or experience like night, with an abstract idea like darkness. Metaphors make symbolic connections with words not physical objects or experiences, such as using the phrase "seeing red" to mean feeling angry. Symbols often have multiple meanings. It is up to us to individually decipher the meaning each may offer us. It is like a personal code. If you've noticed that you're attracted to certain shapes, colors, numbers, or objects, it may be a message from your subconscious with information for your conscious awareness.

Symbols may be universal, cultural, or highly individual. You may attribute universal responses to a shared collective unconscious as proposed by Carl Jung and the transpersonal psychologists or you may feel more in sync with neurobiologists who suggest that certain cues and symbols are embedded in our DNA, probably evolving from survival as a species in the natural world. Maybe you do not see a conflict with the two approaches or have yet another explanation. Regardless your beliefs, symbols are a fun and surprisingly accurate way to explore how our internal processes are being expressed in the world around us.

We often respond to a symbolic association as strongly as if it was the actual stimuli. A famous example of this is Pavlov's experiment when he trained dogs to salivate at the sound of a bell that the dogs had learned to associate with food. To ignore symbols is to be less self-aware and to miss wonderful opportunities to implement symbolic clues and cues to get more of what we truly want in life with less stress and less effort.

Whatever meaning you have attached to a physical symbol, that meaning is activated on physical and emotional levels every time you see it. Using symbolic cues in our spaces is fun, easy, and budget friendly. Once in place, symbols will work for or against you, even if you are no longer consciously aware of their messages. Your subconscious will remember and almost instantaneously trigger what it considers the appropriate physical and emotional responses.

The idea that our homes reflect and influence our behavior, emotions, and health has provided a wealth of worldwide symbolism in literature, myth, art, and many forms of analysis. "Home" is steeped in symbolism. Every aspect carries symbolic meaning: line, color, shape, and features such as foundations, attics, hearths, windows, and doors. Even the word home carries symbolic meaning which is so much more than a physical structure or specific address.

Symbols have been used since ancient times to tell our stories and to help shape our stories by calling in or recognizing and honoring specific experiences or outcomes. Common threads of meaning in color, shapes, line, and abstract symbols have been found across time and cultures. Here are some common associations with numbers of things.

Numbers

Numbers create visual and symbolic patterns. Numbers of things create physical energy patterns, but numbers themselves are essentially symbols. Besides representing specific quantities, numbers are said to be symbolic expressions of common human experiences and traits. The study and use of numerical patterns is found in ancient and modern cultures around the world. Threads of symbolism through numbers have been found in stories, myths, art, and architecture.

Some philosophers and mathematicians believed that numbers hold the secrets of the universe and the psyche of man. There also are many variations in symbolic interpretations that are clearly culturally linked. Are you consciously using any of these common numerical symbolisms in your home?

One conveys independence and leadership. In Western tradition, being "number one" is synonymous to leadership or being the best. One symbolizes the creative spirit, uniqueness. One also is the number of a loner, someone who does not follow the crowd but may set the pace or outcome. In Vietnam, every precaution is taken that the first person to enter the home on the first day of the new year has high moral standards and a solid desire for the well-being of the household, if the household is to receive blessings in that new year.

Two represents partnership and is the number of balance but is also the number of polarity and opposition. "It takes two to tango," "good things come in pairs," and "like night and day" are common Western sayings. Janus, a two-headed Roman god, was able to see both the past and the future and is the namesake of the month of January. In Daoist philosophy, two opposite forces (yin and yang) keep the universe in balance.

Three is often a sacred or magical number associated with taking action. Three is considered lucky. We say, "Third time is the charm." In fairy tales, heroes and heroines are often offered three choices or three tests, finally overcoming their challenges on the third try. In many religious rituals, actions are repeated or performed three times. According to the Mayan Popol-Vuh, it took three attempts to successfully create mankind.

Four symbolizes a balanced and firm foundation, suggesting the stability and boundaries found in rectangles and squares. We recognize four seasons and four cardinal points (north, south, east, and west). In the Bible, there are four angels standing at the four corners of the earth, holding back the four winds of the earth. In Buddhism there are four noble truths. But in the Far East, fear of the number 4 is so common that many apartment and business buildings, hospitals, and hotels skip that room and floor number. In these cultures, four is pronounced like the word "death."

Five is associated with the constant motion of adventure, creativity, change, and social energy. Five is as dynamic as four is contained and stable. "High Five" is a current social gesture of celebratory recognition. Five has been associated with the unpredictable, so be alert when you use it symbolically.

Six symbolizes balanced, harmonious and high ideals. Six represents the feminine principle, the glue that keeps a family or community together. North African Christian philosopher Saint Augustine wrote, "Six is a number perfect in itself, not because God created all things in six days; rather, the convert is true. God created all things in six days because the number is perfect." Jewish mystics used the six pointed Star of David, now the recognized symbol of Judaism. Six is also considered lucky since it is the highest number on dice (The oldest gaming implement known and used before recorded history).

Seven has predictive connotations, a connection to what is to come, and of completion, so seven often has an association to the spiritual. In America, break a mirror and you have seven years of bad luck. In Japan, there are seven Lucky Gods who arrive every New Year with gifts for the worthy. Seven circles form the symbol called "The Seed of Life" which symbolizes the six days of creation with the seventh day of rest in the center.

Eight is a number connected to infinity, spiraling cosmic consciousness, and, more commonly today, with material abundance along with the sense of purpose that goes with it. The symbol for infinity looks like an 8 on its side. In Norse mythology, Odin received eight new rings made of gold every ninth day. Lakshmi, the Hindu goddess of wealth, is associated with an eight pointed star; the points symbolize the eight kinds of wealth provided. In Judaism during Hanukkah, a candle is lit for eight days and children often receive gifts.

Nine is considered a number of completion and is sacred in many religions. Nine has been said to represent a sense of synthesis and humanitarianism, as associated with spiraling wisdom. When multiplied nine always reproduces itself. There are nine months of human pregnancy. In Catholicism, a novena is the act of saying prayers for nine consecutive days. The Double Ninth festival is an old Chinese tradition celebrated on the ninth day of the ninth lunar month. In Taiwan this day is dedicated to senior citizens.

Using specific numbers of things is another way to visually reinforce your goals for a space. How you group things can reinforce or be disruptive for your goals. To get your imagination going, here are a few ideas for your home.

Innergized Tips

- Odd numbers of items tend to be more informal and encourage activity and movement. Even numbers of things tend to be symmetrically balanced and more formal with less movement.
- One of something draws and holds your attention, so use one to create a sense of boundary, like a sentry or marker. When using one of something, make that one thing especially beautiful or meaningful to you. I love doing this with large plants.
- Pairs and twosomes suggest intimacy, partnership, and balance. Two chairs or two night tables with matching lamps, for example, send a message of a stable, equal partnership. Use identical pairs of things for formal balance.
- Three of something creates an active energy pattern. Try three colors or three textures in a room for spark. Use groupings of three things for visual interest. Groupings of three chairs encourage lively social interaction and discussion. Too many items of threes and angular arrangements in a space can seem to "put us on edge" and keep people there from relaxing.
- Four items, such as a set of identical dining chairs, reinforce balance and stability. Like too many squares and/or rectangles, too many items of four can seem boring, rigid.
- Try five torches around the patio placed among six flowering shrubs to represent the dynamic, entertaining possibilities in an area.
- Select a personal goal then select seven photos to place on a bulletin board to represent what you will experience when you have accomplished that goal.
- On a tray, cluster eight items such as memorabilia or photos of what makes you feel blessed and prosperous in life. Or draw the symbol for infinity (eight on its side) and place it somewhere only you know such as behind a piece of art or under your desk lamp. Your subconscious will remember your intention in placing it there and help trigger positive connections.
- Arrange nine beautiful flowers in a vase for closure or to celebrate the completion of a goal.

Numbers of things are patterns you can see, a bit like a secret code in plain sight. Look around your home and see if you can identify any messages your subconscious may be sending you. As with all information, especially when as personal as symbols, only use what resonates with you. Exploring the symbolic meanings associated with particular numbers within your heritage can be an interesting and fun way to tap into the nonverbal imagery of your subconscious or, some may say, the collective unconscious.

Design more for the full experience of being human, adjusting for unhealthy seen and unseen substances and patterns in our homes. Each small step you take to shift to a healthier more supportive environment can help you feel your best and live your best life.

6

Feed Your Heart and Soul

Holistic health is often associated with alternative medicine and healthy eating, but a holistic perspective is all about living a lifestyle that nurtures us as a whole and is not about isolated activities. Your design choices may be a missed opportunity to feed your heart and soul. Is your home comforting and nurturing or full of irritations and toxins? Ask yourself, "How well do my design choices nurture me on a daily basis?"

Current Indoor Health Concerns: Junk Food Design

We are bombarded with information about environmental concerns within our homes. Here, in no particular order, are a dozen research-based indoor environmental concerns found across a slew of literature and online sources.

1. Indoor Air Quality (IAQ)
2. Sleeping Environments
3. Ergonomics
4. Electromagnetic Fields (EMFs)
5. Toxic Load
6. Water Purity
7. Color and Décor Mismatches
8. Building Materials and Finishes
9. Lighting
10. Clutter and Disorganization
11. Acoustics
12. External Contamination

Harmful chemicals in the dust and air come from inside and outside our house. Indoor items like furniture, electronics, plastics, fabrics, cleaning supplies, paint, and even our water can release toxic chemicals, while outdoor pollutants enter on our shoes and through windows and doors. Toxic chemicals have been added to thousands of everyday products including accessories, textiles, and electronics. We live in unprecedented electromagnetic smog. Homes built before 1978 may contain lead paint, a source of lead in dust. A jarring cacophony of unwanted mechanical sounds come from inside and outside our homes, making sound pollution a growing public health concern. Even low levels of chronic air pollution or sound pollution can have a devastating effect on physical and cognitive functioning, especially for our young and those with already compromised health, and on it goes.[25, 50] Home, instead of being a safe refuge in the world, can now seem downright dangerous!

Innergized Approach

Response-Ability

My goal with this chapter is not to frighten you into trying to eliminate everything potentially unhealthy in your home environment. In today's world, that is probably impossible and, thankfully, is unnecessary to significantly enhance your life. With a holistic approach, we have response-ability for our choices and the daily value received for those choices. Stay out of overwhelm by establishing your priorities. Work only with what resonates with you.

Physical aspects affect us directly on the physical level. Less has been written about the psychological and emotional impact of our environments which is the focus of this book. Environmental toxic concerns are complex topics with entire publications and specialized services dedicated to them. Specialists are available to help guide and support us with the specific environmental challenges outside the scope of this book.

After years in the design trenches, I am offering the innergized holistic design approach to help reduce unnecessary life stressors while creating a higher level of vitality and well-being with your design choices. This approach is not so much a fix or cure but a restoration process for a renewed sense of connection to ourselves, the world around us, and more.

Spirituality in Everyday Details

A sense of purpose and connection is closely tied to well-being. Even those of us who do not believe in God or a higher power per se still attach purpose and meaning to our lives. I believe spirituality is more inclusive than a specific set of religious beliefs and need not be compartmentalized into only one area of life. Since we know that nothing can really be separate, spirituality can be found wherever we remember to look for it. You can find the sacred within every part of your home. This is the key to creating truly uplifting spaces.

To help find the sacred amid the ordinary: (1) Remember that nothing is really separate. (2) Set up physical cues and sensory triggers to remind you of what you truly value. Remove or minimize whatever distracts or creates a sense of disconnection from that. (3) Be aware of your daily habits. What draws your time, interest, and energy at home? Is being home uplifting or draining? With new design choices, you can create new habits whenever needed.

Dan Buettner, the founder of Blue Zones, an organization that helps Americans live longer, healthier lives has shared the importance of establishing what he calls the 3 Ps in your environment: Pleasure, Pride (related to self-identity), and Purpose.[51] In essence, the 3 Ps are what gets you out of bed in the morning and they can be supported or challenged with your design choices. After years of research, Buettner has reached the strong conclusion that your environment, i.e., where you live and how you shape your surroundings, is the most impactful thing you can adjust to stack the deck in your favor for a longer, happier life.[51]

Design positive changes with three basic strategies. You can use these strategies separately or in combination. You can (1) repurpose, rearrange, or reorganize; (2) take away, reduce, or minimize; (3) add, enhance, or maximize.

Here is an example of how you can use these strategies. Much has been written about how clutter and disorganization in our homes can result in lost time and money, stress, and family arguments. If you decide these are ongoing experiences you now wish to change, you can: (1) rearrange and reorganize by sorting through the clutter and moving some items to other areas such as seldom used sports equipment to the garage; then group remaining small similar items into attractive baskets; (2) sort through scattered items such as CDs and magazines and donate what is no longer of interest; (3) the storage baskets may be part of a new organization system that includes bookshelves to keep things streamlined and off the floor and end tables.

Pausing to fully experience what is going on in the present moment instead of operating on autopilot is the essence of mindfulness with all of its benefits. Author and meditation teacher Margo Adair said it beautifully, "We tend to forget our connection to the earth, to the sky, to each other, to life that's constantly percolating in and around us. When we forget these connections we wind up feeling drained and isolated. When we remember our connections, we are energized, inspired, and feel a part of all that's around us."

Spatial Patterns

Nature is our best teacher for life-enhancing design. Numerous studies have indicated that humans seem to have instinctive preferences for specific spatial patterns. Some pattern preferences are tied to cultural preferences, yet certain patterns affect us all and have for millennia. It is in our DNA as biological beings. The basic principles are not complicated, but the challenge of listing specific holistic design strategies is the potential for random disconnected application.[7]

Here are my top ten biophilic strategies which have been summarized from multidisciplinary research.[7, 52] All biophilic design guidelines, as with any holistic tips, should be applied when the strategy reinforces other elements for a more integrated and cohesive whole. Think of these patterns as a way of summarizing or joining together spatial patterns that we know can help us.

1. Complexity and Order
   Research indicates that it is the variation in nature and geographic patterns, textures, and colors that brings us the most pleasure. Nature does not match everything in a setting or throughout a day or a year. These patterns have an order, a rhythm, too, but too much sameness in interiors is unnatural and quickly can be sensually boring.

2. Visual Connections to Nature
   This is often accomplished with window views. If nature views are not available, research indicates indoor plants and even art depicting nature can create this connection.[7, 57]

3. Non-rhythmic Sensory Stimuli
   Similar to complexity and order, sensory cues in nature vary and are irregular, not fixed nor static. Think of the sounds of bird songs, a babbling brook, the rumble of a thunderstorm, or sunlight filtering through tree branches as they move in the breeze. For enhanced pleasure and comfort, include unexpected variation in sounds, textures, scents, color, and other stimuli from area to area within your home.

4. Movement: Air-Flow, Thermal Variations, and Water
   While we have attempted to have consistency in air-flow and temperature control, that can contribute to a sense of lifelessness and stuffiness. Addressing this can be as easy as opening a window or adding a small fan for air movement.

   We respond positively to hearing, seeing, and touching water, making water features very desirable in an environment. Lowered stress levels have been quantified by lowered heart rate and blood pressure, enhanced memory, and increased feelings of peace. Plus, moving water generates negative ions. An outdoor water feature that can be viewed and heard from indoors, or a small table top fountain can bring water into your indoor experiences.

5. Lighting, Varied and Diffuse
   Natural lighting changes throughout the day. Those changes are part of our internal clock, known as our circadian rhythm. Harsh, unfiltered, even lighting is unnatural. Pools of filtered lighting as discussed in chapter 4, mimics the effect of being out under the trees and clouds of nature.

6. Natural Materials i.e., Wood, Stone, Branches, Cork, etc.
   In all the countries included in one global study, when elements of nature were incorporated into the workplace the workers' creativity was enhanced.[52] For this pattern, design and decorate with natural materials - or what looks like natural materials and elements - whenever possible.

7. Prospect (Open View/Spaces) and Refuge (Cozy, Sheltered Spaces)
   Prospect is an open setting that provides a quick big-picture understanding of the environment. Open floor plans, wide expanses of windows, and transparent materials all can provide unimpeded views for this sense of prospect. Conversely, refuge provides us the feeling of being sheltered, a sense of privacy and being "cozied in", while still maintaining a connection to the world around us. It can be as simple as a cozy reading chair in a quiet corner where you can deeply relax. Refuge often involves a sense of lower ceilings. A low chandelier over a dining table or down directed lighting can appear to lower the ceiling, contributing to the feeling of refuge.

8. Mystery

   This pattern conveys the idea that there is more to be discovered and draws us into an area with a desire to experience more. Not only is this sense of anticipation pleasurable, a space will seem larger when everything is not immediately seen. One easy way to accomplish this is with a screen or a large plant to partially block the view at the entry or from one area into another.

9. Proportion, Ratio, and Spaciousness

   Spaciousness is a highly desirable spatial pattern for most people and even animals. Many species, including humans, do not thrive when cramped or crowded. A feeling of spaciousness isn't the same as a having a large house. In a spacious home you feel you have room to breathe and move easily. Good storage helps, as does not cramming too much into one area. A sense of spaciousness is all about working with the proportions of a space and within your comfort levels of fullness.

Order verses Clutter

Stress comes not only from too much to do and not enough time, but also from the daily onslaught of stimulation including from emails, cell phones, and all types of information and entertainment. We are bombarded by the importance we've placed on the volume of our belongings along with our growing dependence on technology in a nature-disconnected culture.

Humans have always collected things. We may even be genetically programmed to collect, accumulate, and save things. Before the material abundance of the industrial era, our ancestors had to make everything themselves. They needed to save what could be materially useful. Collecting and storing food was critical to survive long winters and famine. To want more and to keep it may be a common and usually understandable human behavior.

However, in our 40,000 years as modern humans, we have never accumulated so many personal possessions. With postindustrial age material abundance and current information bombardment, clutter and disorganization have been demonstrated to negatively affect our health, emotions and mental performance. But it is your perception of clutter that matters, not someone else's. Clutter is an especially personal issue. If having papers and miscellaneous work related things on your desk doesn't feel like clutter to you, then it's not.

I define clutter as whatever takes away from the function and/or enjoyment of a space. The word "clutter" usually evokes the idea of too many physical things in our home, chaotic piles of papers on the table, or a closet stuffed with unused things. But clutter comes in many forms. Clutter is a distraction that can make it difficult to relax or focus. Clutter can be mildly toxic, somewhat limiting, or downright devastating. As our physical environments become cluttered and disorganized, our thoughts and ideas also can become more scattered or lost, similar to what multitasking does to your brain.[53] Clutter tends to overload your senses, making you feel stressed, and impairs your ability to think creatively. Most of us become much worse at:

- Filtering information
- Switching quickly between tasks
- Keeping a strong working memory

Research is piling up that some people need something of a mess in their surroundings to feel inspired, creative, and productive.

A University of Minnesota study, among others, suggest that the stereotypic messy desk of many geniuses is actually linked to their intelligence and creativity.[54] Psychological scientist Kathleen Vohs summarized it this way: "Disorderly environments seem to inspire breaking free of tradition, which can produce fresh insights (creativity). Orderly work environments, in contrast, encourage convention."

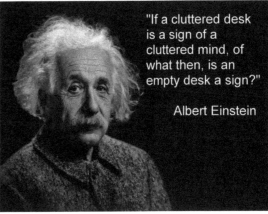

"If a cluttered desk is a sign of a cluttered mind, of what then, is an empty desk a sign?"

Albert Einstein

If your work environment includes some obvious work related messiness like the photo above, left, research indicates you may be gifted![54]

Einstein is among the many creative thinkers and prolific inventors famous for their chaotic work environments. The above right photo includes Einstein's response when asked about his cluttered work environment.

Do you wonder if modern day electronics changes this? Home office photos of Steve Jobs indicates otherwise.

Real life is not always tidy. It is good to be able to navigate through life's messiness. Nature is rich with complexity and a variety of sensory input. Apparent chaos is sometimes healthier and triggers greater productivity than starkness.

But if you are losing time, energy, and your sense of humor along with your car keys somewhere among the chaotic piles, the clutter is working against you. It may be time to consider a change. You achieve a higher quality of life with less stress not more. Neuroscientists at Princeton University looked at people's task performance in an organized versus disorganized environment. The results of the study showed that physical clutter in your surroundings competes for your attention, resulting in decreased performance and increased stress for most people.[55]

During the last thirty years the size of the average American home has grown 53 percent, from 1,500 square feet to over 2,300 square feet. Despite larger homes, according to the Self-Storage Association, Americans spent more than $2.3 billion on storage units in 2014. The U.S. Department of Energy reports that 25 percent of people with two car garages fill them with so much stuff that they can't park a car inside. Of those of us who rent storage units, 65 percent have a garage, 47 percent have an attic, and 33 percent have a basement. So great are our habit and attachment to acquiring stuff, we rent space to hold what we don't want in our homes even though the annual rent is typically greater than the worth of the contents.[16] And we have spawned entire new industries to help us deal with our belongings. Home storage products are reported to have become a $10.5 billion business.

It may seem counterintuitive, but before adding more storage space, try limiting or reducing your storage space instead. With less to sort through, you can more quickly locate what is of value to you because it won't be buried by what is not. When we only keep what we truly need and/or enjoy, our belongings do not take valuable time, energy, and focus from what is really important and even irreplaceable.

Innergized Tips

- Design change with one or a combination of these basic strategies:
  Repurpose, rearrange, or reorganize
  Take away, reduce, or minimize
  Add, enhance, or maximize
- Clear away anything that triggers less than positive feelings. For a literal example, replace chairs that are uncomfortable or need repair. More symbolically, remove gifts you never really liked or now trigger unpleasant memories that do not lift your heart or bring a smile.

- Too much consistency is unnatural. Our pattern-seeking brains are very responsive to novelty and change. Design variety and sensory change in your home. This is especially helpful if you want to change a habit. Change the environmental cues that support that habit.
- A cluttered work environment seems to contribute to nontraditional, creative thinking. Neat orderly environments encourage following the rules, and generosity. Honor what works best for you.
- Collections are especially personal and mentally demanding of your attention. If you have a large collection that you love, consider rotating some of the pieces so you can fully appreciate them individually.
- Every goal has an internal (cognitive, emotional, and sensory processing) and an external (the actual physical triggers) environment to best support it. Design for a higher quality of life by first identifying what you want to experience in your home.
- Life is inherently messy, and not always tidy or comfortable. To be able to tolerate and navigate through the messiness, focus on what helps you live more effectively, not necessarily with concern over how something might look in the moment.
- My personal favorite motivator for minimizing clutter is that getting rid of clutter is estimated to eliminate about 40 percent of housework in the average home, according to the National Soap and Detergent Association.
- WASTE Management aka Clutter Control

Worthwhile?	Do I still need or find pleasure from this?
Arrange?	Can I combine or include this with similar things for easy retrieval in handy baskets for visual clutter control, for example.
Somewhere else?	If seldom used, instead of storing this in my valuable daily space and distracting me from what I need and use regularly, can I find this item somewhere else?
Toss?	What would happen if I lost this in a fire? Would I replace it just as it is?
Entire thing?	Do I really need the entire box of old photos and birthday cards, magazines, etc.?

Keep out of overwhelm by prioritizing your biggest challenges. Identifying any health-related challenges in your environments will help you establish your design focus. Skip over the things you are not interested in addressing at this time. Be kinder to the planet and yourself with simple, cost-effective design changes.

It is time for us to embrace how our homes impact us wholly: body, mind, and spirit. Our home is one place where we can carefully consider the impact of what we include around us and what we want to experience there. You certainly don't need to replace everything in your home or live in an isolated, expensive bubble. Use holistic, mindful design to live more fully, not more constrained.

"One thing we've learned this summer is that a house is not an end in itself, any more than home is just one geographic location where things feel safe and familiar. Home can be anyplace in which we create our own sense of rest and peace as we tend to the spaces in which we eat and sleep and play. It is a place that we create and re-create in every moment, at every stage of our lives, a place where the plain and common becomes cherished and the ordinary becomes sacred."

- Katrina Kenison, *The Gift of an Ordinary Day: A Mother's Memoir*

Section III
Designing A Good Life

7

Special Considerations

Furniture Arrangement

Furniture arrangement is important to aesthetics and far more. No matter how beautiful the furnishings or the architectural features, rooms with poorly placed furnishings cannot function as you want; you may not even want to spend time there. If furnishings are awkwardly placed, both perceived and actual living space is lost and the quality of experiences there is diminished.

Furniture arrangement reinforces where our attention is drawn, how we move through a space, and even how we react and interact with others while we are in that space. Remember that to facilitate desired changes, you can: add or enhance; subtract or minimize; rearrange, redefine, or repurpose your furnishings in a space.

Try these guidelines for arrangements.

1. <u>Function</u>. First, consider function and your intentions for a space. Every goal has an ideal environment that best supports it – both internal (emotions, goals, etc.) and external (sensory cues, physical elements and furnishings). Start any design project with a clear understanding of what you want to accomplish.

   What do you need and want to happen within areas of your home? What activities? When, how often, and with how many people? Is the space primarily for activity or meant to be a space for relaxation or concentration? What has been stopping you? Be as specific with the details as possible, and your design choices become clearer.

2. <u>Focal Points.</u> Next, identify the focal point(s) within the space. The focal point is what draws your attention, where your eye goes first and remains the longest. Windows, fireplaces,

televisions, or any large pieces of furniture such as a bed, can be a focal point. There can be more than one focal point in a room, but one will be the primary focal point. Reinforce the focal point(s) in each room with the furniture arrangement instead of trying to ignore or compete with it.

3. <u>Measurements</u>. You need to know the size of the space and the size of your larger furnishings. Check the doorways and hall measurements, too, to be certain you can get larger pieces into the room. Since the average adult foot is about twelve inches, for a quick estimate you can count your footsteps, walking the space, heel to toe.

   When shopping for new furnishings, take room measurements with you. To be extra cautious before you purchase that new sectional or other large piece, tape the outline of the dimensions onto the floor. Walking around that outline for a day or two should tell you how easy it will be to navigate the area with the new piece in place.

4. <u>Placement</u>. After establishing function, the focal points, and the room and furniture sizes, try these placement tips.

Innergized Tips

To save time, energy, and sometimes relationships, start with a to-scale layout. Use either an online floor planner such as Sketch Up or old-fashioned graph paper to sketch out your desired floor plan with the furnishings to scale. The to-scale layout helps to ensure everything will fit within the space as you imagine and allows you to explore optional arrangements without actually moving furniture around.

- The general rule is to place the largest piece along the longest wall in the room. I sometimes break this rule depending on other aspects in the room. Always explore your options. Place the large furniture pieces first, smaller pieces next, and the art and accessories last.
- Like adding seasonings in a recipe, slowly add furnishings, including accessories, until the desired effect is achieved. Avoid catalog cliché by not trying to match everything. Include a bit of a surprise in some way and use some things that are uniquely you.
- Lighting fixtures are often considered accessories, but a lighting plan should be considered with the basic furniture placement for the best functioning of a space.
- Accessories are fun, personal touches. Many of us want to start with the accessories but they are the finishing touches. Even when an accessory is the inspiration for a space, its job, much like clothing accessories, is to personalize while pulling everything together.
- Balance the visual weight. Grouping large or small pieces into one area or side of a room will make a space feel out of balance.

- Sight lines (how your eyes move over the top of the furnishings) should move over your furnishings in a gentle wave, not in rollercoaster drops. Use accessories such as plants and art to soften any dramatic drops.
- Mix overhead lighting with floor lamps and/or table lamps, and finally add accent lighting, distributing lighting around the room. Effective lighting also means glare control from both natural and artificial light sources.
- Think of the traffic lanes in your rooms as major streets, side streets and alleys. For major traffic lanes, allow at least three feet and six inches for easy movement. Other areas such as between a sofa and coffee table may need less than eighteen inches.
- Avoid lining the walls with furniture; your room will look larger and more interesting. If pulling some furniture into the room looks awkward, unify the grouping with a rug.
- Most of us have too much of everything. For a more open and spacious look, include only what you need, actually use in this space, and still love. You won't miss the rest.
- If a room feels dysfunctional or cold, bring the furniture closer together into a grouping with a clear purpose i.e., conversation, games, television, or reading.
- The recommended height for hanging art (eye level) has many variables. Art and all wall-hung accessories should be balanced with other elements in the room. Most of us have a tendency to hang art and wall accessories too close to the ceiling.
- For a more spacious look, try these strategies: place some furniture on the diagonal. Avoid bold color contrasts. You are not limited to pastels or white walls and furnishings. You can unify a space with mid-tone wall color. Direct attention around the room with lighting.
- People feel more comfortable in square-shaped rooms than in long rectangular ones. Experiment with ways to break a rectangular room into a couple of smaller squares.
- Functional seating arrangement requires a nearby place to set a drink, a book, etc. Side tables should be about the same height as chair arms. Coffee table height should be about the same height as chair/sofa seats or a bit lower.
- For small spaces, choose decor items made from glass, mirrors or other reflective or transparent materials to reflect light and appear light weight, not heavy, in your space.
- Experiment. As HGTV addicts know, even the pros sometimes have to try different arrangements before the room layout seems just right.
- For furnishings that are tired/dated, damaged, the wrong size, or if you just need a fresher look, you have options besides buying new pieces:
     Alter it (paint, slipcover, clean, repair it, or use it in a new way).
     Use color, light, and new accessories to minimize or redirect the attention away from it.
     Sell it and use the money to buy new furniture.
     Move it to another area where it contributes to a fresher look.
     Find creative combinations of any of the above.

Almost always there are multiple ways to accomplish your design goals, including arrangement of the same furnishings within a room. Changing color, pattern, layout, and the accessories can yield very different looks using the same basic pieces of furniture.

Have fun with this - and don't be afraid to make changes as your needs and preferences shift.

It doesn't need to be an expensive complete redesign but your furnishings and how you use them can and should change as you do. Paint, inexpensive accessories, or a new layout can work magic. "Right" or "best" means only the degree to which it is working for you at this point in your life.

"We can't direct the wind, but we can adjust the sails."

- Old folk saying

Floors, Ceilings, Hallways, Windows

Floors

Floors and ceilings together make up about a third of our interiors. They have a huge impact on the overall livability of our space(s). You can use color and the amount of contrast or blending, the variety and the types of lighting, and lines to direct your eye. All can change the apparent dimensions and shape of a room, and even shift the focal points without ever lifting a hammer.

Carpets and rugs can harbor dust, dust mites and allergens, even if vacuumed regularly. The best ways to minimize these allergens are:

(1) Choose a low-pile rug. Flatweave rugs are easy to clean and it's tougher for tiny particles to settle in.
(2) If you don't want a low-pile rug, at least opt for something made of natural fibers such as cotton or wool. They won't off-gas harmful chemicals as much.
(3) Vacuum often and use HEPA filters.
(4) If installing new carpet, try to have it off-gassed out of the home before installation.

When you can see more of the floor, it creates an impression of a larger space. Other techniques that create an impression of more space are:

(1) Use wall-mounted furniture. For example, a drop down table attached to a wall can be ideal for eating or working where floor space is really tight. When not in use, the table then can be folded against the wall to create more room. A wall-mounted shelf is ideal for a snug entry area or as bedroom side tables.

(2) Furniture with slim or tapered legs also allow more visible floor space. Low profile furniture contributes to the appearance of higher ceilings for a more spacious look.

(3) Laying tile or hardwood diagonally draws you into a space visually and can enlarge the appearance of a small room or hallway,

(4) Curving, flowing lines can add interest without taking up limited floor space in tight spaces.

Innergized Tips

- Use area rugs to unify a space or furniture grouping. Do not float a rug in the middle of a grouping. Small throw rugs such as those placed at entrances or in front of the kitchen sink serve functions other than unifying furniture groups. .

- Ideally, all four legs of major pieces should be on an area rug. If this isn't possible, make sure to fit at least the front legs of the grouping on the rug.

- Large tile with few grout lines can help a room look more spacious.

- Consider a low layer of light to show off great floors, to add safety, or to add a layer of interest/dimension. Try tape LED lighting in the toe kick area under cabinetry near the floor.

- For visual "flow" and spaciousness, keep all flooring similar, at least in color tone if not in materials.

- If your flooring is damaged, dated, or you just dislike it but cannot replace it, cover most of it with a large rug, leaving the disliked flooring as trim around the area rug.

- Area rugs can be art on the floor and still ground your room. Such rugs can bring warmth, character, and texture to a room without taking up space. Whether you choose a rug to make a colorful statement or to add subtle texture, a rug can help ground the overall look of an area.

On the left, the diagonal lines of the herringbone pattern on the floor draw you in. An area rug can unify a space and still be interesting art on the floor (right).

Ceilings

Ceilings offer terrific opportunities to change the apparent size and livability of your indoor spaces with design tools of color, contrast, lighting, and line.

Innergized Tips

- Visually raise or lower ceiling height with the use of line and architectural features that draw your attention such as crown molding, built-in shelving, or cabinets. For example, bring cabinets up to the ceiling to add the illusion of more height (with the bonus of storage space for seldom used kitchen items).
- Visually raise ceiling height by hanging window treatments near the ceiling and the room will seem larger.
- If your cabinets don't go to the ceiling and you have no plans to remodel, try lighting on top of cabinets. This bounces light off the ceiling; the ceilings appear higher and the room more interesting.
- Sharp contrasts between the ceiling and wall visually lower ceilings. To lessen color contrast, add at least 10 percent of the wall paint color to the ceiling paint, or paint the ceiling and trim the same as the walls.
- Removing "popcorn" ceilings is a fairly simple but messy job worth the trouble. Smoother ceilings appear to raise the ceiling height, reflect more light, and offer an instant update since this texture for ceilings was popular decades ago. However, popcorn texture often contains asbestos which is a problem when disturbed. Because of the health risks of asbestos, a professional evaluation is a good idea before trying to remove it yourself.
- Low-profile furniture gives the appearance of height. With lower furniture the ceiling will appear to be higher.

Tinted ceilings and horizontal lines help cozy-in this teen's bedroom with high ceilings, (left photo). Cabinets with glass insets and layers of lighting (right photo) make the room seem taller without making it seem heavy.

Hallways

Hallways have an invaluable role in creating flow and connection throughout our homes, although we often ignore them, considering them wasted space. Bring in décor punch and personal style with sensory cues and emotional triggers in your hallways.

Innergized Tips

- Whatever you place at the end of a hallway will draw and hold the eye. So consider the color(s), subject matter and proportion of whatever you use at the end to make sure that the connecting hall area is sending inviting messages and linking spaces.
- If a short hallway ends with a blank wall, hang art with a sense of depth that seems to draw you in such as a landscape.
- Mirrors reflect the light and can make hallways feel larger, lighter, and brighter.
- Narrow hallways feel wider by hanging accessories such as art and mirror frames horizontally. With lower ceilings, try a piece of art with a tall frame to lift the eyes, making the ceiling feel higher.
- Linear lines emphasize and exaggerate the apparent length of long hallways. Rug runners with linear lines, for example, can seem to elongate a hall. If installing new laminate or hardwood flooring, consider laying the boards across the width, not down the length of the hallway as seen below right. Reclaim unused wall space in hallways with built-in book/art display cases, or between-the-studs niches.
- A floor-to-ceiling photo gallery on hall walls is a terrific way to display family photos.
- Color and pattern can work as unifying elements between the adjoining rooms. Wallpaper or tile on walls can be a fun and surprising way to add texture or pattern without taking up floor space.

Whatever is placed at the end of a corridor becomes a focal point, so make it inviting (left). Planks laid across the width seem to widen a hall, while wall color, lighting and architectural features can add interest without taking up limited floor space in corridors (right).

Windows

Windows are often referred to symbolically as a home's eyes. They allow us to visually connect to the world beyond our walls. Windows are essential for natural sunlight and visual connection to the community and nature around us. Window placement and coverings are important for ventilation, climate control, and interior lighting. All these aspects can affect our physical and mental health by reducing stress, medical and utility costs, and increasing our overall comfort while at home.

Doors with glass panels and windows can make a home feel more spacious as well as more connected to the surrounding natural environment and community. The benefits of connecting to the seasons and life's natural rhythms around us are research-validated.

Innergized Tips

- Energy-efficient, double glazed windows can be one of the best home improvements you can make and can provide some major health benefits at the same time. Airtight windows better insulate your home and may contribute to lower noise pollution in your home as well as draft prevention and general climate control.
- Indoor air is often more polluted than outdoor air, so even a few minutes a day to allow for an exchange of air can dramatically improve indoor air quality. Let less polluted air into your home with operable windows to allow the indoor air to circulate with fresher outdoor air.
- One technique to bring more of the exterior landscape and natural light into your room is to use mirrors placed near windows to reflect more of the outdoors into the building.

Window Coverings

Window coverings not only help a room feel finished, they are important to our comfort in a number of other ways. Window coverings can cozy us in, emphasize architectural details, frame a fabulous view, enlarge apparent window size, and even out awkward window placement.

Bedroom window coverings are essential to your health. Blackout coverings are a must to block out the sunlight if you work the night shift or just love to sleep in. Even day sleepers should have window coverings that can be pushed aside and held there easily, to maximize the daylight when when appropriate.

Consider UV rays and the direction of sunlight when selecting window treatments. Too much of a good thing here can increase the utility bills, decrease your comfort, and fade/damage your furnishings. Solar shades now come in a wide array of attractive, organic looks. They are excellent at offering

UV protection for your furnishings, and are perfect for assisting with climate control without blocking your views and incoming light.

Innergized Tips

- Blackout window treatments are highly recommended for all bedrooms.
- Draw attention to a window or a great view with a darker wall color or fabric surrounding the window. Your eyes are drawn to contrast.
- Window panels, which can be stationary or not, can eliminate glare at the window edges and soften the sharp lines.
- Window treatments can be placed outside of the window's actual dimensions to visually balance uneven window placement or to raise the apparent size and height of the window and ceiling, as in the photos below.
- High-quality, thick curtains are a sound investment. Heavy/thick fabric panels assist with sound absorption. They also provide better climate control than only blinds or thin curtains.
- If your window view is nothing to look at, use light filtering treatments to keep the light but block the unwanted scenes as seen in the photo below right.

Before, left, the single living room window needed for natural light overlooks an alley with trash cans. After, right, a light-filtering shade and linen side panels are mounted outside the window's dimensions. This effectively blocks the alley view while eliminating glare, helping with sound control, and helping the window look larger and the room brighter.

photo credit: Michael J. Lee Photogtaphy   www.kirtamdesigns.com

Keep the visual weight in the living area to help a two-story room feel more intimate. Place window panels at the lower level, as in the above left photo for more livable intimacy for two story rooms. Conversely, as seen in the right photo, emphasize impressive two-story volume, take the panels to the ceiling.

Plants as Accessories

Have you noticed? Plants have become the new essential home accessory. If you've checked out almost any design magazine or blog, you've found photos of interiors filled with plants. But plants are more than just an interior design fad. Their increasing popularity is part of the growing awareness of biophilic design, and, specifically, the many ways houseplants contribute to our health. Adding living plants to your interiors is one of the simplest and most cost-effective methods for designing improved well-being within our homes. All plants recycle carbon dioxide into oxygen and help add a bit of moisture back into the air. They can also calm us, helping us breathe easier by bringing some of nature's healing power indoors.

At the same time, more and more of us are rediscovering the beauty of greenery and the many ways plants can enhance the décor of any room. Improved health and aesthetics: a double win! For more on the mental and physical benefits of plants, see Plant Power in the back of the book.

Innergized Tips

- If you are using plants to clean the air, then they should be placed close to where people will be, such as around desks, near seating areas, and as decoration on tables.
- NASA concluded that in a 1,800 square foot house, you should have fifteen to eighteen house-plants in six to eight inch diameter pots to improve air quality. That's roughly one larger plant every one hundred square feet. You can achieve similar results with a couple of smaller plants (four to five inch pots).[56]
- A grouping of plants is more natural and visually appealing than plants rigidly spaced. A grouping can also soften sharp angles and corners in our homes.
- For cognitive rejuvenation, position plants so you have greenery in view from where you normally work. You can also use art and/or a window view of nature's greenery.[57]
- Plants add interest, color, texture, depth, and sometimes fragrance to a room. Even more interest and texture can be added with decorative containers, mulch, and spot-lighting or up-lighting to highlight or cast shadows on walls and ceilings.
- For years, therapeutic gardening has been known to improve cognition and reduce stress. It's reasonable to think there may be similar benefits from activities such as tending desk-sized Zen gardens, bonsai trees, or mini herb gardens.
- Create a wild garden you can see from a window. Landscaping with native plants helps attract local wildlife.
- Save green on your green with cuttings. Many house-plants can be acquired through cuttings. Throw-away vegetable parts such as a lettuce core rooted in water can be the start of a fun kitchen garden for no additional cost at all. For similar ideas, check out the Plant Propagator's Bible by Miriam Smith or YouTube's grow indoor vegetables clips.
- Indoor trees are a great way to bring the outside in. They add a sense of lushness and tranquility along with dramatic aesthetic appeal. Because a tree makes such a big impact, keep the surrounding decor fairly simple.
- Large plants can give an illusion of more space by blurring of a room's edges and suggesting the vistas of the outdoors.
- Terrariums are easy to make in any size or shape wanted and are very low maintenance. If you are not interested in designing your own, complete terrarium kits are available from online sources like Etsy.

- Mold spores thrive in warm, wet dirt. For best indoor air, limit the amount of - and where you display - plants that need a warm, moist soil environment which encourages mold growth. Or bring in some English Ivy which reduces airborne mold among other toxins.

Bromeliads are like exotic flower arrangements but last a long time, unlike cut flowers.

8

Room By Room

Interior design is a young profession with few inflexible rules. Design possibilities are nearly endless. There are now countless publications, tips, and guides, all offering different approaches and advice for specific design topics and styles. Simply sorting your way through it all can feel like a full-time job.

Holistic interior design makes you the ultimate design expert for your home. These general guidelines are meant to help you explore the almost endless options. So jump right in, and get to the good part: living healthier, more effortlessly, and with more vitality and joy.

Entries

Entries are important functionally and psychologically as people transition from the outside world into your personal space. If your front door is not your entry area, what greets you when you arrive home? For many people, that area is dark, cluttered and utilitarian - a garage, mudroom, or laundry perhaps. Wherever your personal entry area is, consider it important. Standing at that threshold, what sights, sounds, and smells welcome you home? For our purposes, include whatever is experienced when first arriving in your space.

A chaotic entry filled with stuff will instantly make your space feel small and uncomfortable, setting a precedent for the rest of your home. Make the first impression of your home calm, organized, and personal. Create a space for a transitional pause. This can be as simple as adding visible cues of what is important to you. Then identify your focal point(s) and display only what brings you pleasure, a smile to your face, or a deep relaxing breath. Keep furnishings to a minimum to keep maintenance simple. Inexpensive washable curtains can effectively cover storage areas as in a garage or laundry room if that is your personal primary entry. A rug by the door can be functional for wet shoes and physically define the space itself.

Entry furnishings that are helpful are sturdy rugs, storage benches, shoe storage, coat hooks, overhead storage like shelves or cabinets, and a favorite piece of art or something personal. What says "welcome" to you? You don't have to have expensive built-in storage units. Design a functional entry inexpensively with department or consignment store finds.

Innergized Tips

- Areas look larger and more intriguing when everything is not seen at once as is sometimes the case in open floor space plans. Explore adding a sense of mystery and spaciousness by partially screening the area with a piece of furniture, a large plant, or a screen.
- If your entry is open to a larger space, decor choices should flow with the rest of the room and into your home. Your entire home should have a thread of continuity but not be perfectly matched or catalog cliché. Just repeat some of the materials, colors or style found elsewhere in your home.
- If you don't have a "real" entry, create one. A shelf or mirror adds interest without using any floor space. A rug should be safe and sturdy enough to weather messy shoes (pun intended). Consider adding a bench with or without a back as a functional room divider and convenient seat for visitors.
- Incorporate as many of the senses as you can. A welcoming scent takes no floor space, but avoid toxic chemicals please. Similarly, minimize any negatives such as old cat litter odor.
- Shoes off at the door is a healthy practice. Use durable mats outside entryways to limit dirt entering the home. Then arrange for an obvious and convenient place for people to leave their shoes near the door.

- Double duty furnishings such as storage ottomans, stools, and benches are invaluable for making the most of limited space.
- In every room, there is an entryway. Those thresholds set the tone for how well the room supports the people who spend time there. Notice what you experience from each room's entry area. Note sounds, smells, lighting, texture, color, etc.

Living Areas

Living spaces are the main areas where people come together in a home. They are hardworking, often multiple-use areas used to receive visitors and entertain guests. Gathering spaces maybe called many names: living room, family room, great room. They could be part of the dining room or kitchen in some homes. Their purpose is to provide a place to be with each other and sometimes to relax alone. The wide mix of activities can be a design challenge.

Innergized Tips

- Make it easy for people to arrive and use gathering spaces. Provide clear pathways to and through the space. You can connect the areas to the rest of the home with clear sensory clues such as lighting, smells, and sounds creating sensory pathways in addition to the literal ones.
- Plan a variety of seating options and flexible configurations as your entertaining needs vary. Consider including versatile multiuse pieces such as ottomans, benches, and stools which can be easily rearranged for extra seating when needed.
- Seating needs to be close enough for a quiet conversation.
- Functional seating arrangements require a nearby place for each person to place a drink, a book, etc. Side tables should be about the same height as the chair/sofa arms.
- Your living room should be able to seat as many people as your dining room. Try a combo of stationary and flexible pull-up seating options so that no one is left standing. Pieces such as storage ottomans, benches, and extra dining chairs can serve as occasional seating.
- Encourage conversation with some seating placed at right angles or in a circular arrangement. Women are more likely to sit side by side (sofa!); most men prefer to sit across from one another. Both men and women are comfortable when seated at right angles or in circular patterns.
- Don't be afraid to invest in a few high-quality accessories or to mix them up with inexpensive finds. Art and other accessories are the personalization that make a space truly yours. Just don't use so many that individual pieces cannot be appreciated or that people are crowded out.

- Consider using a BIG coffee table. A large coffee table in the middle of a seating area can act as an anchor for the room's seating arrangement and even with a display of accessories still have plenty of space for people to set their drinks. A large coffee table is easier to access from all the seating surrounding it. Coffee tables should be the same height as chair/sofa seats or lower.

- People may feel uncomfortable when they cannot see the main entrance of a room or have their back to a public window. If this cannot be avoided, find ways to create a bit of a barrier such as a narrow console table behind the sofa or add a mirror to reflect the entry.

- Ergonomic specialists have discouraged mounting televisions high above a fireplace because of the stress that can place on the neck and shoulder muscles. Experts recommend the top of the screen should be between 15 to 35 degrees from the horizontal plane of your eye level. Aim for 15 degrees.[35]

Sometimes small spaces just need more of the right things, not less (before, left). Here we wrapped open shelving for their art collection around a slim profile fireplace. Yes, this is the same room! A sofa with slimmer lines (not shown) was moved to the opposite side of the room to allow appreciation of the new focal point and for easy flow through and around the room.

Before, left, illustrates challenging seating in a room with little wall space. Circular seating arrangement in the center of the room, after, right, makes better use of available space and gives flexibility for entertaining. The focal wall with fireplace and television we painted dark for emphasis.

Kitchens and Dining Areas

The dining room is for you to gather with friends and family to share the delight of a meal. A kitchen often offers a similar opportunity on a more informal basis. Although a kitchen's main function is food preparation which is essential to healthy eating, kitchens often are also the hub of family life. Dining rooms can also be used for family activities beyond formal dining. Small changes in these rooms can bring unexpected positive returns, including improved nutritional intake by eating healthier at home, money saved on less dining out, and enhanced social experiences of shared meal preparation and dining together. Check out these tips for dining areas and kitchens.

Innergized Tips

- Even with planning, a small kitchen simply can't do everything a large kitchen can, such as serving as a gathering place or a space to do homework. With a small kitchen, first focus on the primary function - meal prep – including any special dietary needs.
- Make it easier to involve other people in tasks linked to food and eating by including kitchen seating if it is at all possible.
- Open shelving offers the opportunity to display pops of color and pattern for visual interest. Remove cabinet doors for easier accessibly. You then can paint the interior a contrasting color to add visual pop.

- Even the smallest kitchen requires a combination of task and ambient lighting. Consider window treatments that can be closed to reduce glare and mealtime distractions.
- Be creative with storage and clutter control. Consider adding a small-scale island, an appliance garage, or a cart that can be rolled out of the way when not needed. Replace standard above-counter cabinets with taller cabinets. You'll get more storage and the extra height will draw your eye upwards, giving the illusion of space.
- Colors of food, healthy vegetation, and white (representing cleanliness), are good colors to include in kitchens. Blue is said to suppress appetite.
- Consider the shape and size of the dining table carefully. Different shapes are beneficial to different family dynamics and goals as we explored in chapter 3.
- Generally, have no more than two extra chairs for the usual number of diners around the table. No additional chairs make it inconvenient to include the occasional guest; more than two extra chairs make it more difficult to create a sense of intimacy for those who are usually present. People may even feel the group is somehow incomplete.

In the kitchen, include both mood and task lighting (above left) so when you've finished the meal prep, you can turn bright task lights down and have lighting more suited to a sociable eating environment, not overly bright or evenly flat. Chandeliers over dining tables give importance to the dining experience and help define the area (above right photo).

Bathrooms

Bathrooms today have been greatly influenced by the spa industry. We want the rest in restroom for a place of pampering, comfort, and relaxation as well as personal hygiene. As with kitchens, cleanliness (real and suggested) is especially important here. In our quest for cleanliness, we sometimes create sterile-feeling bathrooms. A bit of color, something living, and touchable textures adds livability to the hard surface environments of most bathrooms.

Innergized Tips

- If there is little room, think vertically. Add wall niches or open shelves, for example. Wall-hung vanities help a small bathroom seem larger.
- If in good repair but just needing an update, a vanity can be painted or refinished and given new hardware that not only looks good but feels good in your hands. Removing the vanity doors and painting the interior for a splash of color works, as well.
- Excess moisture encourages mold and bacterial growth. Keep the bathroom fan running while showering or bathing and for about fifteen minutes afterward.
- Include nature and natural materials to keep bathrooms from feeling cold and sterile. Consider an English Ivy which loves the humidity and absorbs mold spores.
- Side lighting is best for grooming tasks since all down lighting creates shadows.
- If you have a nice floor consider rope under-cabinet lighting in the toe kick of the vanity. You can also use lighting to highlight special features such as wall niches or a freestanding tub.
- People do not spend lots of time in guest bathrooms, so bold colors can be fun without being tiring.
- Showers can be a wonderful source of tactile and auditory stimulation with the variety of shower-heads and bath bars available today. The water patterns can vary from relaxing to invigorating.
- Soften hard surfaces and add visual warmth with textiles and living plants (right photo, next page). The framed art in the photo (left photo, next page), is actually a sculptured wool rug in the style of one of the owner's favorite paintings.

Whatever the mirrors reflect should be pleasant, a good rule for mirrors anywhere.

Bedrooms

Today, Americans in particular are used to the luxury and privacy of our own bedrooms. This is not necessarily true in the rest of the world. The size of our bedrooms has grown in recent decades to support our desire for some privacy from the rest of the household.

Some people use their bedrooms only for sleeping or intimacy. Some people use awake time there for reading, talking, relaxing, or sharing a drink or a cup of coffee. If space allows, consider creating a sleeping alcove in one portion of the room and dedicate other portions to other uses like dressing. That said, it is best to avoid activities and furnishings for work or exercise which are incompatible with relaxing. If you must include such activities within your bedroom, screen them from the rest of the room.

We tend to focus on our living rooms or kitchens, the places that are seen by guests, and neglect the room where we spend more than one-third of our lives because "no one sees it." But we are impacted by environment even while we sleep. Improving your sleep means more than improving that one-third of your life; the benefits carry over to when you're awake, too. Getting enough quality sleep not only helps you feel and function better the next day, but insufficient sleep is linked with many chronic diseases including diabetes, heart disease, obesity, and depression.[58]

The U.S. Centers for Disease Control and Prevention (CDC) has called insufficient sleep a public health problem, estimating that one in three adults don't get enough restful sleep.[58] Do you have the bedroom of your dreams? Here are tips to help create a rejuvenating bedroom.

Innergized Tips

- Buy the best quality mattress and bedding you can afford. Choose products that are made of organic cotton and wool materials without the chemicals found in most other bedding including mattresses. Your sheets touch your body for eight hours a night so should be of high-quality, soft to the touch, and as chemical free as possible. Look for 100 percent cotton sheets with a high thread count.
- Wool is naturally fire retardant, which means wool items don't require chemical retardants that can be toxic to the skin and the air. While it is important and often a legal requirement for bedding items to have flame retardant, chemical additives, these same chemicals can be dangerous in other ways. Some of these chemicals even increase the toxic gases during a fire; smoke inhalation is the leading cause of death in fires.
- Fabrics are great to help create a quieter sleeping environment. Window coverings, accessories, or an upholstered headboard can all add color, texture, and sound management.
- Carpet is warm and pleasant on bare feet, making it the most popular flooring choice for bedrooms. But carpet retains every speck of dust, dirt, pollen, animal dander and general grime from shoes and feet. If allergies or asthma is an issue, consider replacing carpeting with wood or laminate flooring. If you add an area rug for comfort around the bed, consider organic materials such as wool and use a vacuum with a HEPA filter.
- Studies show we sleep better when the room is cool. Set the thermostat at night at least two to five degrees cooler than what is normally comfortable during the day.
- House-plants not only bring the beauty of nature indoors, they can improve your sleep. Plants such as orchids, succulents, snake plants, and bromeliads emit oxygen at night, making them perfect plants for the bedroom. Broad leaved plants such as dieffenbachia are especially great for additional sound management and adding humidity to the air. Just avoid overwatering your plants which can contribute to allergy triggers of mold and bacteria in the soil.
- Every bed needs a headboard. Footboards or benches at the bottom of the bed are optional, especially when space is tight. In a small bedroom with little space between the end of the mattress and the wall, instead of a footboard, match a bed skirt to your comforter, or use a bedspread that drapes to the floor. The unbroken line of fabric makes your room seem a little bigger.
- Beds should be placed away from busy doorways and drafty windows, if possible. Most of us feel most comfortable with the head of the bed facing the main doorway. Experiment to find what feels best to you in your space.

- Zippered, washable, organic cotton pillow and mattress covers help protect you and your family against dust mites that can aggravate allergies and asthma.

- Minimize electronics in and near the bedroom. Poor quality and insufficient sleep is a serious health concern.[58] Make your bedroom a work and phone free zone for the most rejuvenating space. Use a battery-operated clock for an alarm. Banning blue light sources from the bedroom was explored in chapter 3.

- Pay attention to the first thing you see every morning and the last thing you see every night. How does what you see make you feel? That sets the tone for your day's activities and your evening's slumber.

- Add a bit of romance and another level of relaxation with scent. You can make your own relaxing essential oil sleep spray, as discussed in chapter 3. Lightly fragrance your sheets before bed each night but please avoid all chemical air fresheners.

- Layer your lighting. Wall sconces save space on your nightstand. If you choose ones with swing arms, you can direct the light right where you want it. They are perfect for those of us who enjoy before-bed reading. You'll need at least a couple more light sources. For example, you might include a ceiling light and a floor lamp for layers and balance around the room.

- A bedside table or two is usually a necessity. Identify your needs. If you love to read in bed, a tiny space-saving pedestal may not be large enough to meet your bedside needs.

(Left photo) Nightstands and lamps do not need to match but they should be balanced in visual weight. Chandeliers in the bedroom can add interest and a soft diffused layer of light (above right).

- Toss pillows are an affordable way to quickly update the look of a bedroom. You can swap them out seasonally to mimic the rhythm of nature for a refreshing change.
- Clothing storage needs a plan. Does your closet provide adequate clothing and shoe storage? Do you need extra hanging space, room for folded clothes, or both? Many affordable wardrobe options are available, or you can section off a portion of the room with curtains or a freestanding screen to create a faux closet.
- Select your bedding before selecting the wall paint color. Coordinating paint color with the bedding is easier than finding bedding you love to coordinate with your wall color.
- If you prefer neutral walls, but want some color, add color with art, a colorful rug, or colorful bedding. But remember, muted colors and matte finishes are restful. Bright colors, shiny surfaces, and bold contrasts are energizing, not restful.
- To keep it restful, limit the accessories. A piece of art that you love, a couple of toss pillows, and a scattering of photos may be all you need for the finishing touches. Keep dust-collecting textiles to a minimum if you have allergies.
- Blackout shades or curtains are essential for the best sleep; these tend to cost more, so plan for this investment in your design budget. Mirrored or glossy furnishings and light colors and woods can help lighten up a dark bedroom which might especially appeal to an early morning riser. A too-bright bedroom can be toned down with darker colors and non-reflective surfaces.

Children's Spaces

Kids also want and need a functional bedroom that's personal, a pleasant retreat during the day, and conducive to restful sleep at day's end. Many decorating tips apply to both the master bedroom and kids' rooms. Here are a few considerations especially for the younger set.

Bright colors and clutter are not restful, not even for children. Clutter attracts unhealthy dust in addition to being a visual disturbance to a calm environment. Without easy ways to store possessions, many of us, kids included, simply leave belongings scattered across the room or on the floor, and then clean up by shoving them into a closet or under the bed where items can be lost or damaged. Children's bedrooms, play and study areas all need plenty of accessible storage areas.

When your child is old enough to have regular homework and needs study time, he or she needs a designed area for schoolwork and a different area to unwind. An area for schoolwork can be as simple as a desk, task lighting, and an adjustable chair. For downtime, add a comfortable, fun chair or beanbag. You may plan a study area in a shared area outside of the bedroom such as in the kitchen or at the dining room table. Remember, places to keep books and school supplies will need to be part of the design plan for it to be workable.

Innergized Tips

- A kid's bedroom needs lots of shelves. Be creative with bookcases, open-backed shelving units, or floating shelves mounted directly to the wall; they don't need to be expensive. An old bookcase from another part of your home can be perfect, especially if you paint it a fun, coordinating color before moving it into your child's bedroom. Fasten shelving units securely to the wall to keep them from toppling if your young adventurer decides to climb them.

- Organization is easier by using bins or baskets to keep toys, games, collections, and study materials literally and visually contained. Group similar things together in separate bins and work with your child until s/he knows the system. This makes it easy for them to find belongings and to see where the toys go when playtime is over for the day.

- Baskets and boxes corral and organize the small items. In the early years, use baskets or lidded boxes sized to fit side-by-side on low shelves. This is a good way to store small items like crayons, markers, Legos and other toys with small pieces, miniature animals and dolls, and all the messy, multi-pieced toys popular with the younger age group. When your child is older, the shelves can hold books, school items, collectibles, sporting equipment, trophies, and electronic games.

- For a neat bedroom, you need some sort of closet organizer. For a young child it may be as simple as a closet rod low enough for your child to hang their clothes easily, some shelves or a hanging organizer, and a hamper for dirty laundry. If the closet is large enough, tuck a dresser inside or install a DIY closet organizer with drawers and shelves.

- One or two under-bed storage boxes can be handy. Make your own using old drawers and wheels. Under-bed storage boxes are perfect for storing out-of-season clothing, pads of drawing paper, extra bedding, sporting equipment, or the many collections children tend to enjoy.

- Most kids have passionate interests, however temporary, such as ladybugs, a movie character, or a favorite color. Including your child's favorite subject doesn't take much. A few removable wall decals and a comforter set can be enough to set a personal theme, as in the top following photos. You should be able to easily and inexpensively change the theme when they have outgrown current interests and are ready for something new.

- A shared bedroom does not necessarily mean matching bedding, or even matching furniture. Some children may prefer having a matching room; many may prefer to express their own style. In that case, let each child pick out their own bedding, bedside lamp, and the artwork for their side of the room. Keep some cohesiveness by using compatible colors.

- To reduce potential squabbles or nighttime chatter after lights out, add a bit of distance between the beds by placing a bookcase, dresser, or shelving between the beds as in the upper left photo on the next page.

- If allergies are an issue, keep textiles and clutter to a minimum.

Personalize kids' bedrooms in inexpensive ways that are easily changed as they grow and change. This can be as simple as some paint, removable wall decals and new bedding.

In this play area (left), paint provides contrast and interest; even the curtains here are paint. For a teen's room (above right), a hanging chair provides a fun place to relax.

Home Offices

It's often said about a third of our lives is spent sleeping. Another third of our hours are spent at work. The home office has become an increasingly important consideration.

We often try to compartmentalize our lives, but how well we manage the work portion of our lives also directly affects us financially, emotionally, and socially. It's not just about our overall physical or mental health, enjoying the work you do, being financially secure, or having a healthy social life. It's about all of them because they are all intertwined.

Thanks in part to increases in self-employment, home-based businesses, and flexible working trends for employees, millions of us are choosing to work from home at least one day a week, according to Global Workplace Analytics.[59] Whether you are working for yourself or others, or only require a space to take care of personal record keeping, bill paying, appointment scheduling, and related activities, it is important to have a home office to support creativity, efficiency, and still leave energy to spare.

Recently, there has been an increasing amount of research on biophilic design in the workplace, specifically examining the interactions between workplace design and employee outcomes. Although commercially focused, most of this research is also relevant for effective home offices. A list of natural design components were identified in a recent international study, The Global Impact of Biophilia Design in the Workplace.[52] The top five components include: (1) natural light, (2) views of greenery including indoor plants, (3) sound management, (4) water, and (5) natural colors with bright accents.

This study revealed that such factors can increase general productivity up to 15 percent. Workspaces that inspire, energize, and rejuvenate with natural patterns and elements can improve your productivity and creativity while reducing errors and cognitive fatigue. Cultural differences were seen to influence our design preferences, but the study reinforced the position that many responses to nature are universal, a part of our DNA as biological beings.

A review of research of indoor plants published in the *Journal of Environmental Psychology* reported that indoor plants can boost mood levels, reduce physical and mental fatigue, improve reaction time, lower stress and anxiety, and even boost pain tolerance. Studies revealed that work-related benefits of plants in the workplace include increased feelings of well-being and cooperation, an increase in memory retention up to 20 percent, and an increase in creativity by 45 percent and productivity by 38 percent - all good things whether you work at home, in an office building, or occasionally from a home office.

Innergized Tips

- We don't want home offices to look like offices; they need to be livable and pleasant enough for spending long periods of time there. For many, that means a minimalist design style for a work setting (38 percent).[52]

- Regardless of your preferred design style, the desk and chair need to be a good fit to support your body and work style. A demand for stand-up desks in the commercial environment has flowed over into the home office.

- Much discussion about home office design now focuses on identifying what is essential to do the work well. This involves reevaluation of equipment that is increasingly more compact and versatile.

- Some of us need much more sensory stimulation to work most effectively. Some of us do well with background sounds like a coffee-house environment or an open-plan work area. But some of us do best with little potentially distracting sensory stimulation. Some research indicates that moderate ambient background noise generally enhances thinking at a higher, abstract level, and consequently increases creativity.[60]

- Free downloadable programs and sound machines provide a variety of sounds from coffee-house ambiance to nature sounds. One site that offers free down loadable ambient noise is www.rainycafé.com. As discussed in chapter 3, the ideal sound solution will mask distracting sounds without becoming a distraction itself.

- When considering office clutter, factor in personality traits and working styles. But clutter also can harbor a plethora health challenges, like dust mites. File papers inside a cabinet to control visual clutter, stay organize, and keep dust minimal. Go paperless as much as possible.

- Avoid glare. Don't put a computer screen directly in front of a light source. Avoid overhead lighting directly above computer screens. These lighting placements can create glare resulting in eyestrain.

- Work performance is influenced by personal factors including connecting with your sense of purpose. "Feeling regulators" are what psychologists call items we use to direct our thoughts and emotions. Examples are motivational posters, awards, diplomas, and photos of friends, family, and favorite activities. The idea is to remember why you do what you do. They can be used like a mild self-medication and brought out as needed for an emotional and mental boost. If such items distract they become counterproductive.

- The only bad office color is one you dislike. An accent color of red is associated with an increased performance on tasks requiring cognitively intense focus. The color blue has been linked with increased creativity. Medium green also supports enhanced creativity.[52]

- Office equipment is a huge source of EMFs, positive ions and toxic chemicals. An Earthing pad is one popular option for the office. Shut down equipment if not in use.

- Long concentration on a demanding task even without disrupting environmental factors can lead to mental fatigue and decreased efficiency. Research has verified that having natural elements in the environment helps restore our mental freshness. In academia this is called Attention Restoration Theory. This theory states that when we view and otherwise experience elements of nature a different part of our brain is activated which refreshes our cognitive functioning.[7]

- A variety of lighting sources is a must, no matter how large or small your office. Don't rely on a single source such as overhead lighting or only a desk light.
- Most of us concentrate best facing the room's main entrance. In the photo below left, a large wall mirror (unseen) opposite the desk serves as another window. The mirror, reflects the natural light, the outdoor greenery, and activity otherwise unseen.

David Lauer Photography

Erin Iba Design Associates

Cabinets can keep most office equipment and supplies out of view until needed (left). The bold colors and contrasts in this home office (right) are energizing.

Your workspace may not be confined to one area. Personal workspaces are often part of other spaces, such as in kitchens. Shelves with decorative storage boxes offer a quick transition from work to other activity. Wall-mounted file organizers keep more of the desktop available for work.

Too often we don't take enough time to immerse ourselves in nature or appreciate the living systems that exist everywhere around us. This makes it vital for us to incorporate nature into our day-to-day environments where we spend the most time.

An inspiring, powerhouse home office doesn't need to be costly. Even small steps can make a big difference. By bringing the experience of nature into our workplace, we can create workspaces that support productive work, reduce stress, and restore energy levels - which, in turn, enhance all areas of our lives.

9

A Holistic Way of Life

Holistic Design Summary

A holistic way of life embraces the concept that human beings and the world around us are part of a multidimensional interdependent whole. The holistic perspective integrates multiple layers of meaning and experience rather than narrowly defining human experiences and possibilities. Holism recognizes that we have conscious and unconscious characteristics and both rational and irrational characteristics. We are not just intellect and conscious thoughts. Our multiple intelligence includes insight, rationality, logic, emotion, hunches, gut feel, creativity, a sense of harmony, and rhythm. We can use all of the information available to us to assist us in designing a long, productive, and happy life, starting with our experiences where we spend the most time: home.

In the 1920s, Smuts wrote that instead of matter, life, and mind bring seen as three separate domains, they eventually would be seen as greater emergent wholes with complex interactions. Smuts believed that the compartmentalization of sciences into separate disciplines created limitations to knowledge as well as in the ability to deal with some of the world's most intractable problems.[6] Creating healthier, productive, more connected living spaces is part of that predicted shift today.

An important concept in holistic living recognizes that we all co-create our world. This concept gives us responsibility for our part in the design process. We are encouraged to draw on our inner and outer natural resources and that includes the influence of our surroundings.

Dan Buettner, author of the bestselling Blue Zone book series, gives us worldwide research to support his conclusion that if you set up your environment for a long and happy life, you are more likely to get it. He powerfully summarized, "Your environment is the biggest and most impactful thing you can change to favor your own happiness."[51] We spend more time at home than we do anywhere else.

Regardless of personal backgrounds, home and our ideas of home influence everything that we do. Home not only reflects who we are, it shapes who we are becoming.

My goal for this book has been to make information more accessible to help stack the deck in our favor for everyone open to the powerful resources already around you. Holistic design is all about connection. Not everything will resonate with you. Take what does resonate, and let the rest go. Or put the information into terms that work better for you. Ultimately, the best way, the only way really, to find out how well any of this works for you is to try it.

Our beliefs and our specific needs are as different as our individual homes. But home is a core concept we all carry inside us. Our homes, like other ecosystems, contain webs of interactive relationships resulting in a synergistic whole greater than the sum of the parts. Learn the design principles, identify your goals, and then have fun with a new way of looking at your home. You really can enjoy the process as well as the outcomes.

Some Guiding Principles

- Our attention will always be drawn toward (1) light, (2) color, (3) movement, and (4) bold contrasts. Use these elements to direct attention to what you want noticed. Minimize contrast, bright light, bold color, and movement where you do not want attention.
- Include views of nature, either actual or simulated in art or on monitors, All have a positive effect for us physically and psychologically including faster healing, better cognitive functioning, and more positive moods.
- Incorporate living things and natural materials, actual or symbolic, such as is seen in the shapes and textures of some architectural features.
- Personalize. All of us respond to sensory and symbolic triggers somewhat differently depending, in part, on individual experiences and culturally shared experiences and beliefs. Identify what you need more or less of in your life. Consciously include objects (literal or symbolic) that remind you of what inspires you, brings a smile to your face or a song to your heart, and remove or minimize whatever does not.
- Human designs are often rather uniform, rigid, and angular while nature's features have flow, variety, randomness, and diversity. Incorporate sensory variety of all types. Use lighting patterns, water and fire and/or local colors, textures, and materials for the variety and complexity found in nature.

Here is a recap of some previously discussed examples for sensory cues to calm/relax:

- Muted and pastel colors with soft transitions; blended and/or cool color palettes

- Quiet, repetitive sounds; nature sounds such as flowing water; bird songs or wind in trees; masking or reducing of loud and/or disruptive noise
- Curved or horizontal lines and shapes
- Soft fabrics and soothing textures such as flannel
- Matte finishes and smooth textures
- Subtle/subdued/smaller-scale fabric patterns and solids
- Direct visual connection to nature: greenery and trees through views, artwork, and indoor plants
- Diffused, lower-intensity, warm (yellow) lighting, and layers of indirect light
- Layers and pools of lighting at a color temperature around 2,700 K
- Minimize clutter and disorganization
- Even numbers of things placed in symmetrical arrangements
- Natural scents that physically and/or emotionally soothe such as lavender, jasmine, and vanilla.

Here is a recap of some examples of sensory cues to energize/stimulate:

- Bright colors and bold color contrasts; color palettes of warm colors
- Music with lively varying rhythm; a higher volume of sound
- Vertical and diagonal lines; bold patterns, geometric, triangular shapes, wide bold vertical stripes
- Rough textures
- Hard and/or reflective surfaces such as mirrors, glass, polished metal finishes, and high-gloss paint.
- Views of nature and indoor greenery (physically and mentally restorative)
- Bright, direct lighting with cooler (blue) color temperatures
- Odd numbers of things and asymmetric arrangements
- Movement such as action depicted in art; things or people moving outside your windows or curtains fluttering at the window as from a fan or a breeze.
- Natural scents that physically stimulate such as citrus, peppermint, cinnamon

A large body of research from divergent sciences supports that how we decorate our homes is an underappreciated asset for a long and happy life and stress-less positive change. In general, the more complex, varied, and natural the sensory stimuli in our homes, the healthier it seems to be for us.

Rituals, Intentions, and Blessings

Holistic interior design is about fully experiencing what you have. It is about connection between mind, body, and the world surrounding us. Anchor to whatever helps you feel a stronger, larger connection instead of isolation. Notice how you react and interact within your spaces on a regular basis. Rituals and celebrations can help us stay mindful of and express gratitude for the experiences we are constantly creating within our homes.

Rituals and symbols are found in cultures worldwide and are reminders of what we value. Rituals serve as bridges between ordinary daily life and a larger sense of connection and purpose. We learn them from childhood. Without birthday celebrations, christenings, funerals, family holidays, weddings, and rites of passage, we lose a sense of purpose and connection. Any routine activity at home can be made into a mindfulness practice when you bring your full attention to it. Home offers a wonderful opportunity to experience a sense of connection through the details of your daily life.

Spirituality does not have to be compartmentalized into one area but can be found throughout our lives. Dedicated meditation rooms are great, but there are many ways to incorporate mindfulness into your daily life. Spirituality is found anywhere we look for it. Recognizing this can be key to creating truly uplifting spaces. We all attach purpose and significance to our lives. Body, mind, and spirit blend as we acknowledge a sense of purpose, joy, and connection by how we interact with what we surround ourselves.

Being aware of what you're thinking and feeling can translate to having more options in our daily living. Our habits are a form of ritual. One simple, common ritual is cleaning. Along with any regular cleaning, set a time each year or season to purge your spaces of items you no longer use or no longer mean anything to you - the proverbial spring cleaning to prepare for the new experiences you will be welcoming into your life. A good time for this is your birthday week - or the next new moon - or right now. Simply be aware of how your environment is affecting you, then start with the area that is most bothering you.

Even if you are not moving to a new address, a house warming or blessing is a great way to celebrate the changes you are consciously making in your life and in your home. Housewarming traditions are found around the world. It can be fun to research your family heritage and incorporate some of those traditions into your experiences of home.

Fully Alive

Home symbolizes where you belong in this time on Earth. Home is a place of shelter and acceptance, a place that holds our memories, the promise of our dreams, and our hopes for tomorrow. Your design choices can help you replace habits and emotional connections that no longer work in your life with ones that will. Approach interior design and decorating as you would any aspect for a healthy fulfilling life. The benefits have a radiant effect throughout your life within and beyond your doors.

"This is a journey that we are all on, everybody on the planet, whether we like it or not, whether we know it or not, whether it is unfolding according to plan or not. Life is what it is about and the challenge of living it as if it really mattered."

- Jon Kabat-Zinn, *Coming to Our Senses*

Where you take it from here is up to you. Whatever you choose to do or not do, know that you are already part of the process as well as the outcome. Please do not limit your tomorrows with the overwhelm of today, guilt of yesterday's choices, or the idea that holistic living and a rejuvenating home is a luxury only available to the wealthy. You do not need to replace everything in your home or live in a bubble. Just begin with a focus that strengthens your connections in life within your environment. Focus on designing easy, meaningful ways to live healthier and happier for all of your tomorrows.

Bibliography

Chapter 1

1. "The National Human Activity Pattern Survey (NHAPS): A Resource for Assessing Exposure to Environmental Pollutants," 2001. Klepeis, N. E., Nelson, W. C., Ott, W. R., Robinson, J. P., Tsang, A. M., Switzer, P., Behar, J. V., Hern, S. C., and Engelman, W. H., Journal of Exposure Analysis and Environmental Epidemiology, 11, 231-252.

2. *The Buzz on Buzzwords*, Eco Pulse 2015 Report; Shelton Communications Group.

3. *Drive toward Healthier Buildings*, 2016; Market Report, Dodge Data & Analytics

Chapter 2

4. "Interior Design," Savage, George, and Friedman, Arnold A., 2018, Encyclopedia Britannica.

5. "Work Creates Less Stress than Home, Penn State Researchers Find," Jun 2, 2014, Bernstein, Elizabeth, Wall Street Journal.

6. *Holism and Evolution*, 1926; Smuts, J. C., Macmillan Company, New York.

7. *14 Patterns of Biophilic Design,* 2014, Browning, W.D., Ryan, C.O., Clancy, J.O. Terrapin Bright Green, LLC, New York.

8. "Geomancy and Earth Studies," Stark, Alex, 2018, http://alexstark.com/services/geomancy.

9. "Ecosystem." 2018, www.Wikipedia.org.

10. "A Primer on Green Architecture and Green Design," Dec. 4, 2017, Craven, Jackie, Thoughtco.com

11. ""Sustainable design," 2018, Wikipedia.org.

12. "Stress in America: Missing the Health Care Connection," Feb 7 2013, American Psychological Association.

13. "Stress in America: The Causes and Costs," Pearl, Robert, Oct. 9, 2014, Forbes.

14. "A Place for Learning: The Physical Environment of the Classroom," Phillips. Mark, May 20, 2014, George Lucas Foundation, Edutopia.org

15. "The Cognitive Benefits of Interacting With Nature," Berman, M. G., Jonides, J., Kaplan, Stephen. 2008 Psychological Science. 19: 1207-1212.

16. "The Psychology of Clutter," Flom, Joanne, April 2008, *Chicago Wellness Magazine*.

17. "A Clean Desk," Productivity Institute, Wetmore, Donald, www.balancetime.com

18. *It's All Too Much*, Walsh, Peter, Nov.2007, Free Press.

19. Delos Media Reel, Nov 2 2015, https://www.youtube.com/watch?v=Q5gu_xBaMFQ

Chapter 3

20. "How Many Senses Does A Human Being Have?" howstuffworks.com

21. "Emotional Responses to Multisensory Environmental Stimuli: A Conceptual Framework and Literature Review," Schreuder, E., van Erp, J.B., Toet, A., and Kallen, V. L. @016. *SAGE Open, 6* (1).

22. "The Olfactory System," U.S., National Library of Medicine.

23. "The Smell of Virtue: Clean Smells Promote Reciprocity and Charity," Liljenquist, Katie, Zhong, Chen-Bo, and Galinsky, Adam D., 2010, Psychological Science 21(3)381-383.

24. "Noise," thefreedictionary.com.

25. "4 Surprising Facts About Noise Pollution,"2018, www.wallmark.com.au/news/4-surprising-facts-about-noise-pollution.

26. "Burden of Disease from Environmental Noise," 2011, World Health Organization.

27. "Noise pollution is a bigger threat to your health than you may think, and Americans aren't taking it seriously," Lee, Nathaniel, Anderson, David, an Orwig, Jessica, Jan. 2018, businessinsider.com.

28. American National Standards Institute, Standard No. 53.5. Federal Standard 1037C.

29. American National Standard for Telecommunications Standard T1.523.

30. "The Many Colors of Sound," Neal, Meghan, Feb 16 2016. The Atlantic.

31. "How Walking in Nature Changes the Brain," Reynolds, Gretchen, Jul 22 2015. *New York Times.*

32. "Can Music Help You Calm Down and Sleep Better?" National Sleep Foundation. sleepfoundation.org.

Chapter 4

33. *Color, Environment, and Human Response*, Mahnke, Frank H. John Wiley & Sons, Inc., 1996.

34. "How LED Lighting May Compromise Your Health." Mercola, Joseph, Oct 23 2016, Mercola.com.

35. "Visual ergonomics at work and leisure," Long J., and Richter H., 2014, WORK 47 (3): 419-420.

Chapter 5

36. "New View of Mind Gives Unconscious an Expanded Role," Goleman, Daniel, Feb 7, 1984, *New York Times.*

37. "A Field View of Reality to Explain Human Interconnectedness," June 13, 2016, heartmath'org.

38. "Electromagnetic Fields," 2018, National Institute of Environmental Health Services (NIEHS).

39. "What Are Electromagnetic Fields (EMF)?" World Health Organization (WHO), 2018

40. "Something in the Air: What you don't know can hurt you," Spector, Paul, Sep 3 2017, huffingtonpost.com.

41. "Reducing Electromagnetic Frequency Exposure May Improve Your Health," Genser, Julie, Apr 2, 2008, naturalnews.com.

42. "Earthing: Health Implications of Reconnecting the Human Body to the Earth's Surface Electrons," National Library of Medicine, Chevalier G., Sinatra S. T., Oschman J. L., Sokal K., Sokal P., Jan 2012, Journal of Environmental and Public Health.

43. "Electric Nutrition: The Surprising Health and Healing Benefits of Biological Grounding (Earthing)," Sinatra S.T., Oschman J.L., Chevalier G., Sinatra D., 2017, Sept 23, Alternative Therapy and Health Medicine (5):8-16.

44. "The effects of grounding (earthing) on inflammation, the immune response, wound healing, and prevention and treatment of chronic inflammatory and autoimmune diseases," Oschman, J. L., Chevalier, G., Brown, R., Mar 24 2015, J. of Inflammation Research, 8, 83-96.

45. *Earthing: The Most Important Heath Discovery Ever.* Ober, Clinton, 2010, Basic Health Publications.

46. "Negative Ions Are Great for Your Health," June 24, 2016, BodySoul.com.

47. "Negative Ions Create Positive Vibes," Mann, Denise, May 2002, www.webMD.com.

48. "Air ionizers wipe out hospital infections," McDowell, Jan. 2003, NewScientist.com.

49. "Holistic Health," medical-dictionary.thefreedictionary.com.

Chapter 6

50. "Toxic Air Pollution Can Penetrate the Brain: Study," Worland, Justin, time.com.

51. "3 Science-Backed Habits That Will Help You Live A Longer and Happier Life," Buettner, Dan, July 2018, marieforleo.com.

52. "HUMAN SPACES: The Global Impact of Biophilic Design in the Workplace," Cooper, Cary, Browning, Bill, 2015, interfaceinc.scene7.com.

53. "What multitasking does to our brains," Widrich, Leo, June 12, 2014, bufferapp.com.

54. "Tidy Desk or Messy Desk? Each Has Its Benefits," Vohs, Kathleen, Aug 2013, Psychological Science.

55. "Scientists find physical clutter negatively affects your ability to focus, process information," Doland, Erin, March 20, 2011, Unclutterer.com.

Chapter 7

56. *How To Grow Fresh Air,* Wolverton B C, 1997, Penguin Books.

57. "Integrating the arts into healthcare: can we effect clinical outcomes?" Kirkin, D., and Richardson, R., editors, 2003, *The Healing Environment Without and Within*, London: RCP, pp 63-79.

Chapter 8

58. "Sleep and Sleep Disorders," Centers for Disease Control and Prevention. Division of Population Health, Feb 22, 2018, cdc.gov/sleep/index.

59. "Telecommuting Trend Data," Jul, 2018, globalworkplaceanalytics.com/2017-state-of-telecommuting-in-the-us.

60. "Is Noise Always Bad? Exploring the Effects of Ambient Noise on Creative Cognition." Mehta, Ravi, Rui, (Juliet) Zhu, and Amar Cheema *Journal of Consumer Research* 39, no. 4 (2012): 784-99. doi:10.1086/665048.

Plant Power

61. "Particulate matter accumulation on horizontal surfaces in interiors: Influence of foliage plants," Lohr, V.I. and C.H. Pearson-Mims. 1996. Atmospheric Environment 30(14):2565-2568.

62. "Ornamental indoor plants in hospital rooms enhanced health outcomes of patients recovering from surgery." Park S H, Mattson R H, Sep 15, 2009, Journal of Alternative and Complementary Medicine.

63. "6 Mental health benefits of plants: Does plant power boost your mood?" Simon, Adam, Sep 10, 2018, pushdoctor.com

64. "Houseplants Can Make You Happy Study: Caring for Plants improves quality of Life," Zerbe, Leah, Oct 13 2008, rodalewellness.com.

65. "Office plants boost well-being at work," University News, Jul 9, 2013, University of Exeter.

66. "How to grow your own fresh air," Kamal Meattle, ted.com/talks.

Plant Power

Indoor plants may be best known for their ability to remove indoor airborne toxins and particulates. NASA research indicates placing at least one potted plant per every one hundred square feet of floor space can dramatically improve air quality.[56] All plants do this to some degree, especially those with broad leaves. The NASA researchers found that plants absorb airborne substances through tiny openings in their leaves, but roots and soil bacteria are also part of the air purification process.

Scientists are discovering even low levels of air pollution can have chronic and sometimes deadly impact. Some fatal, long-term health effects include respiratory diseases, heart disease, and cancer. Did you know that air pollution has been linked to Alzheimer's and other degenerative diseases? [50] According to the EPA, our indoor air is often significantly more polluted than the air outside, making indoor air pollution a top health concern, especially for the young and those with already compromised health.

It seems prudent for all of us to try to improve indoor air quality at home even if symptoms are not currently noticeable. Skip expensive air purifiers with filters you must keep replacing and filter the air naturally with beautiful living plants. Plants can remove air pollutants like benzene (a leading cause of cancer and anemia), formaldehyde (that causes certain types of cancer and irritation of the skin, eyes, nose, and throat), and xylene (that causes headaches, dizziness, and respiratory difficulty).[56]

Houseplants offer benefits to nearly every organ in our body, including the brain. If all that's not motivating enough, here are more good reasons to include plants in your home.

Breathe Easier During photosynthesis, plants convert the carbon dioxide we exhale into the oxygen we need, thus increasing indoor oxygen levels. This opposite pattern of gas use makes houseplants and people natural partners.

Reduce Noise Levels Plants absorb and deflect sounds through their leaves, resulting in more peaceful places to relax and unwind. Broad leafed plants are especially good at noise reduction.

Interiors Feel More Spacious Blurring the edges of a room gives the area the appearance of being larger than it is. Plants and indoor trees bring in the depth of open spaces and outdoor vistas.

Bring a Room to Life Plants add vibrancy to sometimes lifeless interiors. Plants come in a wide range of colors, textures, and scale to literally and figuratively add life to your spaces. Create a focal point in an otherwise boring area with an indoor tree or grouping of smaller plants.

Reduce the Dust A Washington State University study found that 20 percent of house dust was reduced with plants, important for health, less cleaning, and even beauty.[61] Other research has established a link between airborne pollutants like dust contributing to fine lines and facial wrinkles so less dust in the air, more youthful skin!

Help You Heal Faster In one study, hospital patients with a view of greenery or flowers in their rooms, reported less anxiety, needed less pain medication, experienced fewer complications, and were discharged sooner. Scientists speculate that by reducing stress hormone levels (cortisol) and improving mood, views of greenery help enhance the healing process.[62]

Some plants have first-aid benefits. For example, Aloe Vera is great first-aid for burns. Calendula heals wounds and soothes skin, and chamomile soothes an upset stomach. With little cost, plants can give you a living and self-replenishing first aid kit.

Improve Mental Health Caring for something living can be great therapy if you're depressed or lonely. Pets are not always an option but plants are a great alternative. Research also has shown that the presence of plants leads to increased feelings of calm, a marked improvement in self-esteem, and increased feelings of optimism and control.[63, 64]

Humidify the Air Plants are natural humidifiers, adding moisture into the air we breathe, which is helpful for dryness of the skin, throat, nose, and lips and helps ward off cold and flu symptoms.

Better Sleep Just looking at plants calms us, and the scents of lavender and jasmine plants are proven to enhance a state of tranquility. Consider a nighttime oxygen adding superhero like the snake plant aka mother-in-law's tongue for more restful sleep throughout the night.

Improve Creativity and Productivity A University of Exeter study revealed that plants in the workplace increased creativity by up to 45 percent and productivity by 38 percent. Plants also have reduced cognitive fatigue, the number of errors, and stress levels. Studies show that having plants around can increase concentration and memory retention by up to 20 percent.[65]

There is a perfect plant for everyone and every interior environment. Views and pictures of trees and nature's greenery will also work, even for lowering stress, heart rate, speeding up healing, and enhancing mood. Of course, you can receive the benefits from plants by simply going outdoors. But if you can't get out in nature as often as you'd like, bring the restorative power of nature indoors. Add houseplants or sit by a window and look out from time to time. No window or no view? Use art for your view with much of the same psychological benefits.[57]

Some of the hardest-working plants NASA identified for indoor air purifying are listed here: [56]

Spider Plant: This common household plant could be considered an essential for every home. NASA ranked this decorative, easy-to-grow houseplant as one of the best for air purifying.

Boston Fern: The Boston fern often is cited as the most effective plant for removing airborne toxins, removing more formaldehyde per hour than any other air-purifying plant.

Garden Mum: The garden mum is outstanding at removing indoor airborne contaminants such as ammonia and formaldehyde when kept indoors in pots.

Golden Pothos: This hardy houseplant is a good choice for those with less than a green thumb. It's also exceptional at removing carbon monoxide and formaldehyde, two common airborne toxins.

English Ivy: As an indoor houseplant, English ivy reduces the amount of mold spores in the air as well as other indoor toxins, according to the American College of Allergy, Asthma and Immunology.

Rubber Tree: This long-lived tree is a good general air purifier and releases high levels of oxygen. An easy plant to grow, it can thrive in dim lighting and cooler areas.

Wax Begonias: Technically a succulent, this plant is loved for its bright flowers and waxy leaves. They are good at removing airborne benzene, a toxin common in furnishings adhesives, and building materials.

Peace Lily: The peace lily is a low maintenance beauty that's great for relieving irritation and illness triggered by many airborne toxins, especially benzene and acetone commonly emitted in household items from paint to electronics. It is a good choice for a home office area.

Weeping Fig Ficus: A weeping fig is a tree that can survive well indoors. This beauty is great for removing ammonia, formaldehyde, and xylene from your indoor environment.

Areca Palm: These palms are among the top plants on NASA's list of air purifying house-plants. They do wonders for removing xylene and formaldehyde from the air.

Snake Plant. This easy-care plant, also known as Mother-In-Law's Tongue, does well with low light and absorbs carbon dioxide and releases oxygen during the night while most plants do during the day. Add one to your bedroom for a clean-air oxygen boost at night.

Aloe Plant. Well known for its healing properties, aloe can also monitor indoor air quality. When amounts of airborne toxins become excessive, aloe leaves will develop brown spots.

Kamal Meattle discusses how we can *grow* clean *air* with three commonly available plants, shown below.[66]

| **Areca Palm**
Chrysalidocarpus lutescens | **Snake Plant**
Sansevieria trifasxiata | **Money Plant**
Epipiemnum aureum |

India's 2008 groundbreaking fifteen year-long study used NASA research and these three common houseplants: areca palm, snake plant (mother-in-law's tongue), and money plant. The study found that the building now has the healthiest indoor air in New Dehli. Specifically, compared to other buildings in the city, the building showed reductions of:

- Eye irritation by 52 percent,
- Respiratory conditions by 34 percent,
- Headaches by 24 percent,

- Lung impairment by 12 percent and
- Asthma by 9 percent,
- Energy costs were reduced by 15 percent, and
- Worker productivity showed an increase of 20 percent.

Scent-Sational Superstars

Artificial air fresheners can be overpowering and toxic. Many plants add wonderful natural aromas that do not add to dangerous indoor air pollution even as they delight us visually with their texture and color. Here is a sampling of a few of my favorite scent-sational superstars.

Citrus trees: Orange, lemon, lime, grapefruit are all are surprisingly easy to grow indoors with enough sunshine, and can reward you with sweet smelling blossoms and can even yield fruit. Your best bet is to choose a dwarf, grafted variety like Meyers Lemon.

Cuban Oregano: This is an easy-to-grow, big leaved, attractive, edible bush with a spicy aroma. Cook with the leaves or just enjoy the scent when you brush by. This plant can thrive outdoors in the summer.

Eucalyptus: Famous for its unique scent, eucalyptus can be pruned to keep it full and bushy indoors. Foliage can range from dark green and purple to a soft gray green.

Hoya: Hoyas are easy-to-grow, old-fashioned vines that are back in style. Many have waxy, sweetly scented pink or white flowers. The glossy, dark green leaves make attractive vines in hanging baskets even when it's not in bloom.

Jasmine: Both jasmine and lavender are renowned for their relaxing, sleep enhancing fragrances. Jasmine relapolyanthum, has an aroma that is especially fragrant at night and it is easier to grow indoors than lavender. Vigorous climbers, they need a trellis or support.

Mint: All types of mint are fragrant when brushed and are fast-growing. Most form large, lush patches with leaves that are easily harvested for culinary use. Corsican mint is small in size but big on fragrance; small low-growing bright green leaves cluster to resemble a moss carpet.

Orange Jessamine: This bushy delight has long-lasting white flowers that smell like orange blossoms and has beautiful and fragrant foliage even when not blooming. The aroma is subtle.

Rosemary 'Arp': This hardy shrub-like herb with gray-green, needle-like leaves releases a distinctive lemony-pine smell when brushed. Its fragrant leaves are great for cooking and are considered a natural insect repellent.

Scented Geranium: These easy-to-grow plants come in a wide range of subtle scents: mint, pineapple, nutmeg, apple, orange, rose, and more. Some have fuzzy leaves that are as fun to touch as smell. Both leaves and flowers can be used in cooking to flavor jellies, cakes, butters, tea, etc.

No green thumb? No problem. Like pets, plants vary in personalities and needs. For success with any houseplant, you need to match the right plant to the right environmental conditions. Some plants need more attention than others and some are toxic to cats and dogs. If plant allergies plague you, stay away from certain houseplants that are known to trigger allergies for sensitive people. Frequent offenders are weeping figs, ivy, palm trees, and plants needing more humidity. Start with a spider plant, rubber plant, or snake plant; these all have forgiving natures and are difficult to neglect to death while they make life a little better for us.

Sound Management Exercise

The role of sound in our homes is easy to underestimate or disregard. Yet sound and patterns of sounds can bring cellular transformations affecting blood circulation, nervous and respiratory systems, metabolism, and the endocrine glands in positive *or* negative ways. Sounds can encourage or discourage social interactions, introspection and relaxation, and other daily activities.

Sit quietly in each room of your home and listen.

(1) Describe what you hear. Do you hear sounds that are loud? Soft sounds like a hum or a whisper? Are they irritating? Stimulating? Soothing? Intermittent, continuous, or rhythmic? Be as descriptive as possible.

(2) If you do hear sounds, from where are they coming? If you hear very little, how does the silence make you feel?

(3) As you walk through your home, what kind of sounds do your footsteps make? Do the sounds of footsteps vary from area to area? How do doors opening/closing sound?

(4) How does the experience of walking through your home make you feel? Does your response vary at different times of day, for example late at night?

(5) Do you experience variety in the type of sounds you experience throughout your home?

(6) Remembering the ABCs, list some ways you can reduce any unwanted sounds.

(7) If there are areas "too quiet for comfort," what are some ways you can add pleasant sounds to those spaces?

Suggested Reading List

For anyone wanting a little more around theoretical foundation, here is a list of books I've found inspirational, or to be good resources, and sometimes they are equal parts fun and informative.

Biophilic Design: Theory, Science and Practice of Bringing Buildings to Life by Kellert and Heerwagen
Geared toward architecture and healthcare facilities this is a good overview of biophilia, a term coined in 1985. The book includes photos and worldwide projects of all sizes that can enhance human well-being by including nature and its patterns, thereby creating healthier indoor spaces.

The Biology of Belief by Bruce Lipton
Lipton, a cell biologist and research scientist, discusses how even our individual cells are responsive to their environments and are in constant interaction. The epigenetics discussed is an evolving science changing our understanding of the link between mind and matter. Whether or not you agree with all of his conclusions, this easily read book is a game changer for many of us.

The Blank Slate: The Modern Denial of Human Nature by Steve Pinkner
Drawing from science and logic, Pinkner replaces the blank slate theory with the concepts that: our common nature springs from our common biology, is not very malleable, is not a social construct, and that our individual and cultural differences, while undeniable and marvelous, are smaller than what we have in common as human beings in our shared physical world.

Color, Environment & Human Response by Hank Mahnke
Mahnke was a pioneer in perceptual analysis of environmental situations, especially within the field of color. Written primarily for design and architectural professionals involved with the planning and design of public facilities, this book is not necessarily a fun read but offers some intriguing information for us all.

Coming to Our Senses: Healing Ourselves and the World through Mindfulness by Jon Kabat-Zinn
This is one of several great books by an author known for his work as a scientist, writer, and teacher dedicated to bringing mindfulness into the mainstream of medicine and society.

Evolution in Four Dimensions: Genetic, Epigenetic, Behavioral and Symbolic by Jablonka and Lamb
Complex yet accessible, the authors synthesize the rapidly evolving social and biological research, including how environment affects us as individuals and as a species.

The Feeling of What Happens: Body and Emotion In Making Consciousness by Antonio Damasio
Written by a neuroscientist, this book reviews where consciousness research is today, how we absorb and respond to the world around us, and why this is important to all of us.

Healing Spaces: The Science of Place and Well-Being by Esther Sternberg
Sernberg explores the relationships between the senses, the emotions, and the immune system, supporting theory with empirical evidence. Geared for health institutions, this is still a good overview of how the things we see, hear, and experience in our environments affect our mental and physical health.

Home: A Short History of an Idea by Witold Rybczynski
A bit dated, this classic is still a good overview of how our ideas of what we call home have been shaped. Rybczynski, also an architect, urges us to "reclaim home from the architects" to make home personal and fulfill our need for domestic well-being.

House Thinking: A Room-by-Room Look at How We Live by Winifred Gallagher
Gallagher draws on behavioral science research, interviews with architectures and designers, and cultural history as she guides us through rooms in a traditional American home and explores how our homes actively influence our thoughts, feelings, and actions.

How To Grow Fresh Air by Dr. B. C. Wolverton
NASA research discovered that common houseplants make the best indoor air purifiers including for the hundreds of airborne chemicals commonly released from furnishings, carpets, building materials, and more, making our indoor air more pollinated than outdoor air. This book reviews the research and then is a guide to choosing the right indoor plants for you and your home.

Human Universals by Dr. Donald Brown
Brown explores physical and behavioral characteristics that are considered to be universal among all cultures. These universals include art, symbolism, myths, and legends.

A Natural History Of The Senses by Diane Ackerman
This easy read explores the human senses from perspectives such as biology, art, and human consciousness. The message is that the sum of our senses is more than the individual parts.

A Pattern Language by Christopher Alexander
A classic built on the tradition of pattern books used by designers and builders from the eighteenth century onward, this book focuses on the psychological benefits of patterns and the three-dimensional spatial experience rather than the aesthetic focus of previous pattern books.

Seeing Is Believing: An Introduction to Visual Communication by Arthur Asa Berger
Berger explores how images evoke feelings. The emphasis is on mass media but the information is relevant for all of us.

Snoop: What Your Stuff Says About You by Sam Gosling
Read this best seller to "boost your understanding of yourself and sharpen your perceptions of others through clues of what our work and living spaces can reveal about who we are in a glance." Gosling's popular book full of research and supporting stories is being further supported by emerging research.

CPSIA information can be obtained
at www.ICGtesting.com
Printed in the USA
BVHW061922300822
645851BV00015B/609